The Encyclopedia
Taekwon-Do Patterns

*The Complete Patterns Resource For Ch'ang Hon,
ITF & GTF Students Of Taekwon-Do*
Volume 1

CheckPoint
Press

The Encyclopedia Of Taekwon-Do Patterns

The Complete Patterns Resource For Ch'ang Hon, ITF & GTF Students Of Taekwon-Do

Volume 1

By Stuart Anslow

Warning

This book contains dangerous techniques which can result in serious injury or death. Neither the author nor publishers can accept any responsibility for any prosecution or proceedings brought or instituted against any person or body as a result of the use or misuse of information or techniques described or detailed within this book or any injury, loss or damage caused thereby. Some of the techniques and training methods described in this book require high levels of skill, control and fitness and should only be practiced by those in good health and under the supervision of a qualified instructor.

The Encyclopaedia Of Taekwon-Do Patterns

The Complete Patterns Resource For Ch'ang Hon,

ITF & GTF Students Of Taekwon-Do

Volume 1

By Stuart Anslow
2nd Edition

Photographs by Kate Barry, Colin Avis & Stuart Anslow

Cover and Chapter Graphics by Jonathan Choi & Liam Cullen

Cover & Interior Layout by Stuart Anslow

Proof Read & Edited by Lyndsey Reynolds

Secondary Proof Reading by John Dowding

British Library Cataloguing In Publication Data

A Record of this Publication is available

from the British Library

ISBN 978-1-906628-16-1

First Published 2010 by

CheckPoint Press, Dooagh, Achill Island, Co.Mayo, Republic of Ireland,

Tel: 00353 9843779   www.checkpointpress.com

For Gill,
my "Chon-Ji"

Acknowledgements

I would like to express my gratitude to the following students and instructors of our wonderful art who have helped turn this collection of books into a reality.

First of all I would like to thank many of my own students who were involved in this project, some in multiple roles; Kate Barry and Colin Avis who both assisted me in taking the thousands of photographs, as well as being in them. Lyndsey Reynolds who proof read every page and posed for the Silla Knife Pattern chapter; Vikram Gautam, Parvez Sultan, Sushil Punj, Marek Handzel, Richard Baker and Jonathan Choi who all posed for various chapters as well, with Jonathan editing many of the various poses that accompany the start of each chapter, along with Liam Cullen (a friend rather than one of my own students) who also edited the graphics for the book covers, which is work that I could not do myself, as my initial attempts were poor to say the least.

I extend my gratitude and sincere thanks to my friends and fellow instructors Gordon Slater and Elliot Walker who posed for some of the chapters in these books, as well as John Dowding who performed a secondary proof read for me. Mr Slater also authored a great forward for this book series.

A big thank you to Master George Vitale, a true Taekwon-Do historian and researcher, for his most in-depth historical piece on the 'True' and 'Complete' history of Taekwon-Do, commissioned especially for these books (which can be found in appendix v, on page 248), as well as his help with research into the patterns, which along with Dani Steinhoff's research (thank you Dani) I was able to combine with my own to publish what I believe is the most definitive history of those Taekwon-Do pioneers that were involved in the actual creation of the individual patterns. I am very grateful to Gerald Robbins, creator of the Taekwondo Hall of fame website (www.taekwondohalloffame.com) for allowing me to use photographs from the site so that I could include as many recent photographs of these legendary pioneers as possible.

I would also like to express my appreciation to my friends; Yi, Yun Wook for assisting me in the correct hangul translations for each pattern, as well as the book title hangul and various bits of terminology. I am grateful to Master Paul McPhail (ITFNZ) for allowing me to use his work on the various motions employed by the ITF as well as a study on the sine wave and my friend Piotr Bernat for his help regarding the Global Taekwon-Do Federation (GTF) patterns featured in these books.

I extend my thanks to Master Keith Yates for clarifying the patterns of Grandmaster Jhoon-Rhee, Kevin McClear for clarifying the correct order of the patterns practiced by students of Grandmaster Hee, Il Cho as members of the Action International Martial Arts Association (AIMAA) and Daniel Gaul (Chun Kuhn Do) for clarifying the Kihap points used by Grandmaster Kim, Bok Man.

I also wish to thank a number of people who have contributed indirectly to this book, by either clarifying certain points for me, clarifying terminology or contributing in other ways. These people are Master Parm Rai (ITF), Master Ha Xuan (GTF), Master Earl Weiss (ITF), Stephen Gell (GTF), Art van der Lee (Oh Do Kwan), Patrick Steele (ITF), John A. Johnson (ITF), Philip Hawkins, Joseph Marrero, Chris Spiller (ITF) and Paul Mitchell (TAGB) - I thank you all as your input has shaped these books in some fashion.

Of course, I couldn't conclude these acknowledgements without thanking my instructors, David Bryan and John Pepper who set me on the right path and taught me most of the patterns I now practice and teach myself. And of course all those who helped pioneer the patterns founded by General Choi, Hong Hi, as well as Grandmaster Park, Jung Tae and Grandmaster Kim, Bok Man for the patterns they further devised, developed and instituted.

Foreword By Master George Vitale, 8th Degree

It is my pleasure to write this foreword for Mr. Stuart Anslow's latest gem, a book series on Taekwon-Do patterns. Mr. Anslow, a talented and dedicated martial artist and black belt instructor has made a name for himself in the martial art world as a steadfast defender of Taekwon-Do's ability to provide sound self defence skills to its students. The basis for his claim, which I steadfastly agree with, is to return to the roots of Taekwon-Do, when it was developed in the Republic of Korea's Army as an effective military means for self defence. This was during a period when strong defence skills were necessary to survive on the rough streets of Korea and during the protracted periods of war time that Korea was engaged in. The effectiveness of this new Korean martial art, a compilation of the fighting systems available at the time (1950s and 60s) has been well documented on the field of battle as well as reported in the periodicals of the day.

The soldiers who originally developed this Korean martial art were led by a legendary Major-General and Ambassador Choi Hong Hi, one of the founding members of the ROK Army. Gen. Choi over his lifetime (1918-2002) devised 25 patterns, called Tuls in Korean. These martial art 'forms', as many call them, are comprised as Gen. Choi would say, of "various fundamental movements, most of which represent either attack or defence techniques, set to a fixed and logical sequence". According to Gen. Choi training with these patterns will improve flexibility of your movements, build your muscles, assist with body shifting, help with one's breathing, develop fluid motions and allow for rhythmic movements that are aesthetically pleasing. Finally he felt that patterns provide a "critical barometer in evaluating an individual's technique".

Training with the patterns has become an important part of Taekwon-Do's syllabus for both promotion and competition. Additionally to not only helping to develop technical proficiency, diligent study and practice of these patterns is needed to help the student grow their mental or spiritual discipline. Adherence to the strict instruction of one's master instructor or the established criteria of competition allows the student numerous opportunities to enhance character traits necessary to build discipline. Knowledge of the meanings of the patterns and the great Korean patriots and significant events in Korean history that they are named after, also affords each student with fine examples to mentor and strive towards, which assists in developing their individual character further.

General Choi not only developed the original Taekwon-Do patterns, but he had the foresight to name them after these figures and events so details of Korea's history and culture would not only be spread around the world, but would be safeguarded against eradication, in case Korea ever suffered under the brutality of an occupying force again, as they were disseminated globally through his Taekwon-Do. These patterns became an important part in making his Taekwon-Do a distinctly Korean martial art. They, like other martial art forms, Katas, Poomsae or Hyungs, help to define their art. The Chang Hon patterns are like Gen. Choi's signature. Signatures are unique and much like another patriot, John Hancock, who signed America's Declaration of Independence in a large, bold way, allowing him to stand out during their late 18th century struggle for freedom. This is his fingerprint, his legacy, what he left behind as a gift for mankind for all of eternity. The 24 patterns he left us with reflect 24 hours, one day, or all of his life that he lived in the 20th century and into the next millennium.

These books cover not only the 24 patterns left to us by General Choi, but also Ko-Dang as well. This Tul, at times referred to as the lost pattern is contained within this work. The only other books to do this to my knowledge is the Patterns Handbook published by the United States Taekwon-Do Federation, which contains text instructions only and Hee Il Cho's Volume 3. The 39 moves of this pattern however are captured in this work with both photos and diagrams, in addition to the all important written instructions. Of course the older books written by General Choi contained just four of them in 1959 and only 20 in 1965. His other later books published through the International Taekwon-Do Federation (ITF) contained just 24, either with Ko-Dang or Juche, with none of them containing the detail that is presented here.

There have been other books on the Chang Hon patterns like the series of 5 books by Jhoon Rhee that only covered 9 color belt Hyungs up to red belt level. Hee Il Choi's series of 3 books still contain only the first 20 patterns developed by Gen. Choi and his soldiers. Never before have all 25 been covered in such detail. Additionally the 3 fundamental exercises required for promotion and advancement 4 direction punch, 4 direction block for 10th gup white belt beginners and 4 direction thrust for 2nd kup red belts are included as well.

These books also contain the Silla Knife pattern created by Grandmaster Kim Bok Man. Grandmaster Kim was a Sgt-Major under the command of Gen. Choi in the ROK Army. He was a member of the historic Taekwon-Do demonstration team that first took Taekwon-Do abroad when they toured Vietnam and Taiwan in 1959. Sgt-Major

Kim also went to Malaysia in 1963 where he helped General Choi finalize 16 of the Chang Hon Tuls. He was responsible for helping Taekwon-Do spread through out South East Asia. This pioneer was also a founding member of the ITF in 1966 and now teaches his art of Chun Kuhn Do.

Finally Mr. Anslow's series of books feature the patterns devised by the late Grandmaster Park Jung Tae, often referred to as the People's Master and used by the Global Taekwon-Do Federation (GTF). It is believed that no other book contains these patterns. So this work is a great resource for GTF students, who also do the ITF patterns as well. Grandmaster Park was a key right hand man to General Choi throughout the 1980s, as the former ITF Secretary General and Chairman of the ITF Instruction Committee. He was instrumental in creating Juche, Taekwon-Do's final pattern and the most Korean of all of the original Tuls.

Stuart has included Kihap points as emphasized by various groups or instructors. His true history section helps to sort out the confused and muddied story of Taekwon-Do's development. He takes the time to credit the original pioneers for some of their many contributions, so his books are most inclusive, as should be and as few, if any are. The studies written by Master Paul McPhail, one of the ITF's most technically savvy researchers, will help students understand the ways of motion, that are often confusing and hard to understand.

As an instructor Stuart Anslow teaches and focuses on Chang Hon Taekwon-Do. He does not get bogged down by organizational constraints or the politics that often can be in play. Therefore his work transcends these boundaries. In the words of a Pioneer Grandmaster Rhee Ki Ha, instrumental in assisting with the development and the spread of Taekwon-Do worldwide and the first person promoted to IX Dan (9th Degree) by the principle founder, Gen. Choi, we are ITF, "International Taekwon-Do Family". These works, along with his previous work are major steps forward in uniting this original Taekwon-Do family. Unity within the Tae Kwon Do community is long overdue. When one studies this recent project and his past contributions, it becomes increasingly clear that we have so much more in common than that which separates us. We are after all one Art and in addition we share aspects with all Martial Arts. Unity among "ITF stylists" should come first, followed by all Tae Kwon Do groups. Then it will be easier to see how we are all "just martial artists". These books, like Mr. Anslow's previous works on the hidden applications of the patterns is a must have for any serious martial artist.

Foreword By Gordon Slater, 6th Degree

Patterns, Kata's, Forms, Drills, whatever you want to call them are a basis…a foundation of many of the martial arts in the present and the past.

So what are the benefits of performing and perfecting of patterns? Some will say; *"It is a method of putting individual techniques into a logical sequence, it is building muscle content to perform techniques, improving ones stances and applications. It is a attacking and defence system."*

I explain to my own students; *"Patterns are like learning a foreign language, each technique is an individual word within that language, but to speak the language you have to put the words into sentences, Patterns are forming those sentences to enable you to speak the language, perform the art."*

Like all traditional martial arts, Patterns have been handed down from founder to student, who eventually becomes a Master, Master to instructors, instructors to senior students and so on. Also like all martial arts in our modern world, splits occur within organisations. How big would the founding body that first came to these shores (the U.K.) be today if it were not for all the splits and the birth of new organisations?

Today many martial arts schools are becoming independent, or merely affiliated to other larger groups to allow some recognition. And then there is evolution, some groups have changed techniques within the patterns or modified them. Some have stayed with tradition. I am sure Masters could debate the pros and cons of change and tradition until the end of time.

"If it is not broken why fix it?" Vs *"If one doesn't change, one gets left behind."*

What I am trying to point out here, is the evident dilution of the patterns gene pool. Different groups many have a slight difference (or big difference depending how they view it) in the performance of different patterns. What this book had tried to encompass is most people's views. It is unbiased, it does not judge the rights and wrongs of each difference in start position, finish position, speed of technique, where to Kihap, sine wave, hip twist etc.

What it does do is try and show all Taekwon-Do styles a logical way of performing each technique. These books demonstrate, in printed form, extensive photographic sequences of all the Ch'ang Hon patterns. Use it as a guide, use it as a bible, use it how you wish. Right or wrong opinions collected together give you a better understanding of anything i.e. Politics, the best system of an attacking football team, how to get from A to B the quickest route etc. View this book with an open mind, please do not be blinkered.

Mr. Anslow has spent many an hour sourcing information and different opinions to enable him to produce these volumes. He has sought out Masters and students alike to get their views, and ask the questions of 'why and how?' in order to define the small differences and make them as accurate and applicable to all as possible. With all this knowledge, he has then burnt much midnight oil in putting it all together, something many of us want to do, but never quite get around to. Therefore I have nothing but praise for Mr. Anslow in his tireless work to produce these volumes. A job very well done. Congratulations!

Finally, with regards to rank. My views are; *"A belt does not say how good you are, only what grade you are."*.

"Don't dismiss an opinion because of rank, 40 years experience doesn't always mean they have the greater knowledge."

If you judge a person on indepth knowledge opposed to time served, then from my opinion Mr. Anslow is of Master status!

Thank you Mr. Anslow for allowing us to share your knowledge!

About The Author

Stuart Anslow received his black belt in the art of Taekwon-Do in 1994 and is now a 5th degree.

He is Chief Instructor of the renowned Rayners Lane Taekwon-do Academy, which was established in 1999 and is based in Middlesex, UK.

During his martial arts career, Stuart has won many accolades in the sporting arena, including national and world titles. His Academy is one of the most successful in the country winning numerous gold medals at every martial arts championship his students enter, a testament to his abilities as an instructor.

In 2000, Stuart won a gold and silver medal at Grandmaster Hee Il Cho's 1st AIMAA Open World Championships in Dublin, Ireland and in 2004 he returned with 14 of his students to the 2nd AIMAA Open World Championships where they brought home 26 medals between them, 7 of them becoming World Champions in their own right, 2 became double world gold medallists, all from a single school of Taekwon-do.

In 2002, Stuart founded the International Alliance of Martial Arts Schools (IAOMAS) which drew martial artists from around the world together, growing from a few schools to over 400 in under a year. This non-profit organization is an online student and instructor support group that gives travelling students the ability to train at over hundreds of affiliated schools worldwide and is truly unique in the way it operates.

Stuart has been a regular writer for the UK martial arts press, having written many articles for *'Taekwon-do and Korean Martial Arts'*, *'Combat'*, *'Martial Arts Illustrated'* and *'Fighters'* magazines, as well as taking part in interviews for some of them. His numerous articles (which can now be found on the Academy web site) cover the many related subjects of martial arts from training to motivation, but his main love is Taekwon-do.

As well as his Academy, Stuart is the Chief martial arts instructor for two local schools (one private, one comprehensive), one of which was the first school in the country to teach martial arts as part of its national curriculum.

In 2002, Stuart received an award from the Hikaru Ryu Dojo, a martial arts academy in Australia, presented by their Chief Instructor and fellow IAOMAS member Colin Wee when he visited Stuart's Academy in the UK. In recognizing Stuart's contribution, Colin stated (referring to IAOMAS) that *"nothing to date has been so foresighted and effective as Stuart's work in establishing this worldwide online martial arts community."*

In October 2003, Stuart was inducted into the world renowned Combat Magazines *'Hall Of Fame 2003'* for his work within the field of martial arts on a worldwide level. Combat magazine is the UK and Europe's biggest martial arts publication.

In 2004 he was selected as the Assistant Coach for the Harrow Borough Karate team, to compete at the prestigious London Youth Games held at Crystal Palace and has held this position ever since. During the same year Stuart also received various Honorary awards for his work in the International field of martial arts. From the USA he received a *'Yap Suk Dai Ji Discipleship'* award for his innovative work within IAOMAS and *'T'ang Shou'* society award for promoting martial arts on a worldwide scale.

In 2006 he was presented with a *'Certificate Of Appreciation'* from the members of IAOMAS Canada which read *'In recognition of your un-dying contribution to the evolution of martial arts and your inspirational and innovative formation of the International Alliance Of Martial Art Schools'*. Though just a humble instructor or student as he refers to himself, he continues to inspire others.

Also in 2006 he released his first book relating to Taekwon-do; *'Ch'ang Hon Taekwon-do Hae Sul: Real Applications To The ITF Patterns'* which explored the applications of patterns techniques contained within the Ch'ang Hon patterns, away from what was considered the *'norm'* for applications in favour of more realistic (and ultimately more beneficial) techniques. The book was extremely well received and became an instant success, seen as a 'must have' by both instructors and students worldwide.

In 2009, his love for Taekwon-do and disappointment with the coverage in the various Taekwon-do magazines led him to publish his own online magazine *'Totally Tae Kwon Do'*; a free, downloadable magazine for all students of the art. Supported by his friends, Tae Kwon Do instructors and students around the world it too became a worldwide success.

Stuart is well known in the UK and internationally and apart from being a full time instructor of Taekwon-do, teaching at local schools and running Self Protection courses for groups associated with his local Council, he is the father of four beautiful children, one with Downs Syndrome, whom he supports and cherishes to the best of his ability, despite his hectic work schedule.

Though a full time instructor, his reputation is gained not only by his own career but also by his uncompromising approach to teaching and the standards within his Academy and that of his students. The students quality are testament of his 'no short cuts' approach to how martial arts in general and Taekwon-Do in particular, should be taught. His classes flourish with quality students despite much local competition from schools with a more *relaxed* approach to teaching and gradings. Many of his senior students feature in the photographs within this book.

Chloe, Callum, Logan and Jorja Anslow

Table Of Contents

Introduction

Originally it was my wish to produce a single book covering all the patterns in the Ch'ang Hon system, but sadly it was not to be as the cost would have been too prohibitive, so it was divided into three volumes.

So this series of books has come together to be a comprehensive reference for all students of Taekwon-do that follow the Ch'ang Hon system originally devised by General Choi, Hong Hi, including those that parted ways during Taekwon-do's history to date. This means they are suitable as a reference guide not just for those in the ITF (International Taekwon-Do Federation), but for those in organisations that are no longer connected to the ITF, such as the USTF, GTF, UITF, GTI, TAGB, AIMAA, BUTF, PUMA or indeed any Organisation, Federation, Association, Club, School, Academy or group that follows the patterns listed in this book; *The Ch'ang Hon Patterns*, *Blue Cottage Forms*, *ITF Patterns* or *Chon-Ji Forms* as they are also known. These books also include the Global Taekwon-Do Federation's Hyung's (the preferred term of Grandmaster Park, Jung Tae) and Silla knife pattern; patterns which were created or devised by pioneering instructors along the same lineage stemming from General Choi and are thus now part of the Taekwon-Do worlds collection of patterns.

Taekwon-Do's history stretches from before 1955 (when it was actually named) to the present and a consequence of this is that there are various styles of the art which were the pinnacle of the Ch'ang Hon system at certain points in time. For example, a student who's instructor started teaching in the 1970's and continues to teach the way he was taught will learn and perform slightly different from a student who's instructor started in the 1990's or one that is very current with any ITF changes. When writing these books I wanted to take this into account, so rather than simply show things the way I teach or learned them I enlisted help from some instructors that have come from different lines to me and thus perform their patterns slightly differently and as such, the various time periods are represented as well. As the books are designed to be an encyclopedia for all students of Taekwon-Do rather than students from a particular organisation I felt it was a good idea to have the various stages/differences represented. Throughout the book, the students and instructors that pose for the various photographs have performed, trained and/or taught patterns within the UKTA, ITF, GTI, TAGB and BUTF and as well as independently, thus representing a large portion of students throughout the world who perform them in a similar manner.

The Taekwon-do world has many organisations, each having minor differences with how they do things. For example, one organisations L-Stance may be slightly different in width than another's or some will execute a Forefist Punch using 'hip twist', while others will use 'sine wave' etc. and so the differences in *basics* can be numerous. However, all organisations that can trace their roots back to General Choi have one constant and that is the patterns themselves; as although an L-Stance may be of a slightly different width, or the way they move between techniques may be different, in the main, with a few minor exceptions (which I have tried to note in these volumes), the actual techniques each organisations students execute within each of the 25 Ch'ang Hon patterns remain pretty much the same. It is with this in mind that I wrote these books. It differs from other books of this type as it doesn't tell you how you *must* perform the basics (though it gives examples) or how long or wide your stances *must* be or whether to use sine-wave or hip twist, it simply tells you what each move is, what stance it is in and just as importantly, how to get from one technique to another.

Over the years there have been many good books published on the Taekwon-do patterns, many of which I own. Indeed General Choi himself has written both the 15 volume encyclopedia, as well as a condensed version. However, the former is expensive and hard to get and the latter only details the patterns in text form, with few pictures, neither of which contain the pattern *'Ko-Dang'* which many Taekwon-do students are required to learn and practice. Consequently, those books that do contain *'Ko-Dang'* do not contain the pattern *'Juche'* which again, many students need to learn and practice. In some organisations *'Juche'* replaced *'Ko-Dang'*, while others never instituted *'Juche'* to begin with. To complicate matters more, years later, some organisations once again replaced *'Juche'* back with the original *'Ko-Dang'*, with one organisation renaming *'Juche'* to *'Ch'ang Hon'* (ICTF) and another renaming it to *'Ko-Dang'* (ITF under Grandmaster Choi, Jung Hwa) despite keeping all the moves the same. These books include both *'Ko-Dang'* and *'Juche'* to cover this gap.

Furthermore, some of the earlier released books while good, only contained the first 20 patterns but over the years, General Choi developed a total of 25 Ch'ang Hon patterns and this book includes them all. These books also include the 3 Saju exercises he developed which rarely appear in other books. Only *Saju Jirugi'* and occasionally *'Saju Makgi'* have been documented in other books, but these books also include *'Saju Tulgi'*.

Some pioneering instructors who once helped developed the original patterns went on to institute or develop their own. In order to make this book collection a true *Encyclopedia Of Taekwon-Do Patterns* I have included these as well. Apart from the historical merit these patterns have, it is important for those students in the GTF (Global Taekwon-Do Federation) as they have to learn 30 patterns in total and as yet, I haven't seen any books that show them at all, so I hope I have done them justice. These are the six *'Jee-Goo Hyung'* developed by Grandmaster Park, Jung Tae. Though some simply call them the *new GTF patterns* others refer to them as *Jee-Goo hyung* because *Jee-Goo* means *Global.*

I have also included the *'Silla Knife Pattern'*, instituted by legendary Taekwon-Do instructor Grandmaster Kim, Bok Man because it is one of the most requested patterns I have come across on various Taekwon-Do internet forums, possibly because some schools wish to add a weapons form but want one that is Korean based with the added benefit that it comes from such a pioneering instructor. Grandmaster Kim, Bok Man instituted many additional forms for his own students, both empty handed and weapon based forms but the *Silla Knife Pattern* is the only one which is mentioned. That said, I would have liked to include more, but space did not permit it so I have represented this great master with the Silla Knife Pattern.

Aside from having a complete collection of patterns in a single set of books, a small bug-bear of mine is that previous patterns books often show individual pictures of each move within each pattern (of the ones they cover), from the point of view of an examiner watching you. This is fine (and is the way I have also laid out these books) until the student is travelling back to his or her start position and facing away from the examiner, where by many books simply show a photo of the pattern performers back and you cannot even see the technique at all - this has been corrected in these volumes as most techniques have a full size, forward facing shot.

One of the biggest problems I have seen with virtually all *'step by step'* pattern books is that while decent, they are not really a true *'step by step'* guide. They simply show each technique at its final stage, then the next and the next etc. but they never actually show you how to get from one to another, how to execute the actual technique fully, the chamber positions and how your feet move with the various spins, pivots and slides. This for many students is very confusing. In these books I have tried to correct this by showing the movements from one technique to another by way of multiple pictures of the performer moving between techniques and nearly every technique is covered in this way.

Coupled with the *'step by step'* photographs, each movement is described in text form, along with directional arrows and detailed foot diagrams, showing both previous and current foot positions to make it even easier for the first time performer of a pattern to grasp them. On occasion, when one *count* is actually two movements (for example move #12 of Hwa-Rang tul is both a Side Piercing Kick and a Knifehand Strike), these have further been split into 'A' and 'B' shots in order to show the performance of the whole movement.

These volumes also list many of the minor differences in various organisations, such as the various motions used by the ITF, Kihap points for those that utilise them, the actual order of patterns organisations require and a sine wave study.

As part of this book I wanted to have a section on the history of the patterns and pay homage to those that helped in their creation. Most know that General Choi, Hong Hi always had the final say on the patterns contained within his system, but many others helped devise them (to various degrees) and they have never been given full credit, so part of this book finally acknowledges their contribution to the patterns of Taekwon-do. I also wanted to include a 'History of Taekwon-Do' section, but as these books relate to just the patterns I included a 'Brief History' at the beginning of each volume, but also a more complete history section as an appendix in volume 1, which is possibly the most concise and researched, not to mention true history ever to appear in a Taekwon-Do book that isn't a history book per se.

Finally, I have not listed specific applications within these volumes because; firstly I know that when a student passes a grading and needs to learn a new pattern, the actual applications are very much secondary to learning the *pure* techniques of the pattern themselves. This is what I refer to as *'stage 1'* of patterns training, with *'stage 2'* being learning them in-depth, with as much detail as possible, which this book also covers. *'Stage 3 and 4'* are learning, applying and training realistic applications which are covered in the book *'Ch'ang Hon Taekwon-do Hae Sul: Real Applications To The ITF Patterns'*. Secondly, the sheer amount of information within these books on the patterns alone means there was little space for discussing applications anyway. As these are covered in my other book it seemed ultimately pointless trying to squeeze applications into these volumes. In any event, the ITF (as well as other organisations) already have various applications to the movements contained within their own patterns. Those who have already read *'Ch'ang Hon Taekwon-do Hae Sul'* will know my personal views regarding this particular issue, so I wouldn't feel comfortable listing standard applications as portrayed in certain other books. Finally of course, this series of books are for learning and performing solo patterns.

This first volume features all the Kup grade patterns in the Ch'ang Hon system of Taekwon-Do, used by both the *International Taekwon-Do Federation* (ITF) and other *Ch'ang Hon* based organisations, as well as the *Global Taekwon-Do Federation* (GTF) patterns required at coloured belt levels. It also features all the *saju* exercises and the first of the black belt patterns; *'Kwang-Gae',* therefore taking the student from complete beginner all the way to 1st degree black belt. I hope you find them a useful reference tool.

A Brief History Of Ch'ang Hon Taekwon-Do

Contrary to popular belief, Taekwon-Do is not a 2,000 year old Korean martial art and its connection to the ancient Korean art of Taek-Kyon is tenuous at best. It is in fact derived, for the most part, from Shotokan Karate. It also has other martial arts (such as Judo, Hapkido, Boxing, Wrestling and even Chinese Martial Arts influences) fused into what is now know as 'The Art of Hand and Foot' aka Taekwon-Do.

In 1945 Korea was liberated from the Japanese and Korea officially formed its armed forces (its modern military). Although Japanese martial arts remained being taught in Korea (by Korean instructors) in the various Kwan's (gyms), General Choi, Hong Hi wanted to break away from the arts of Japan, to have a martial art to train his soldiers in that had Korean values and at the same time instil national pride following the devastating effects of his country being occupied by Japan. He had learned Karate in Japan during the occupation of his country and had been teaching it to the soldiers under his command since 1946.

General Choi, Hong Hi

President Syngman Rhee

In 1954 during the Korean war, President Syngman Rhee saw a demonstration by the military Korean martial arts masters under General Choi's leadership and was so impressed he ordered that it be taught to all military personnel. This blessing from the president propelled Korean martial arts forward like a rocket. General Choi is known to have been teaching martial arts to his 29th Infantry Division on Cheju Island already and in 1954 he founded the Oh Do Kwan (Gym of My Way), along with Lieutenant Nam, Tae Hi, which was seen as the catalyst for the formation of Tae Kwon Do, as while General Choi taught the soldiers Karate he was, at the same time, formulating Taekwon-Do

A unification effort was made to unite the various Kwans that were teaching in Korea, in order to make them a

Colonel Nam, Tae Hi

unified single Korean martial art and despite opposition, the art was officially named on the 11th of April 1955, known as the birth date of Taekwon-Do, a name put forward by General Choi. Despite this, for many years only General Choi's soldiers in the Oh Do Kwan and their civilian counter parts in the Chung Do Kwan used the term 'Tae Kwon Do'.

Photograph from the meeting when they named Taekwon-do with many martial arts masters present. General Choi can be seen at the head of the table. circa 1955

Naming this emerging art was simply the beginning, in fact even when officially named not one of the patterns were fully formulated, though in 1955 the first Ch'ang Hon pattern (Hwa-Rang) was finished. Over time Tae Kwon Do moved further away from its Karate roots by devising more new patterns, named after Korean historical figures or events; emphasising the rising and dropping into techniques (which was later termed sine-wave) as opposed to the Karate way of keeping the head the same height throughout; and of course introducing many more kicking techniques. Eventually, Taekwon-Do broke the chains of its roots and became distinct in its own right.

Even though Taekwon-Do has evolved into a martial art for all, including a large sport based side, it should be remembered that it was formulated as an art of self-defence, by soldiers, for soldiers and its effectiveness was no more evident than when it was actually used on the battle fields of Vietnam, where it was so feared by the Viet Cong that soldiers were told to avoid engaging in combat, even when Korean soldiers were unarmed, due to their knowledge of Taekwon-do![1]

Taekwon-Do is one of only a few martial arts that have a proven, battlefield tested, track record. Following the battle of Tra Binh Dong,[2] Times magazine ran an article that stated *"It was knife to knife and hand-to-hand—and in that sort of fighting the Koreans, with their deadly tae kwon do (a form of karate), are unbeatable. When the action stopped shortly after dawn, 104 enemy bodies lay within the wire, many of them eviscerated or brained"*[3] .

(On the night of St. Valentine's Day, a North Vietnamese regiment of 1,500 men struck at the 254 man Korean Company.)

It was knife to knife and hand-to-hand and in that sort of fighting the Koreans, with their deadly (a form of Tae kwon Do), are unbeatable. When the action stopped shortly after dawn, 104 enemy bodies lay within the wire, many of them eviscerated or brained. All told, 253 Reds were killed in the clash, while the Koreans lost only 15 dead and 30 wounded.

—Time— 24 Feb 1967

'A Savage Week'. Time Magazine, 24 February 1967

1959 was an influential year for Taekwon-Do as well as the start of the Vietnam war. The Korean Taekwon-Do Association (KTA) was formed, an armed forces demonstration team toured Taiwan and South Vietnam and General Choi published his first book on the art of Taekwon-Do and in 1962 the first Taekwon-Do tournament was held.

1962 was also the year that General Choi was forced to retire from the military due to his lack of support for President Park, Jung Hee who took power following a bloodless coup in 1961. Instead, General Choi was made an Ambassador and shipped off to Malaysia where he continued to teach and formulate Taekwon-Do, which included formulating 15 more Ch'ang Hon patterns.

General Choi finally returned to Korea in 1964 only to find that, due to politics, the Korean Taekwon-Do Association (KTA) had ceased to exist and had been replaced with the Korean Tae Soo Do Association (KTA) which was formed in 1962. However, in 1965 General Choi was elected as President of the KTA and managed to return the name to the Korean Taekwon-Do Association. He also published his second book on Taekwon-Do and lead a demonstration team around South East Asia and Europe. This demonstration tour was called the 'Kuk Ki Taekwon-Do Good-will Mission'!

On the 22nd March, 1966 General Choi formed the International Taekwon-Do Federation in Seoul, South Korea, with Master Kim, Jong Chan designing both the ITF badge (logo) and the ITF flag.

---

[1] 'Captured Viet Cong orders now stipulate that contact with the Koreans is to be avoided at all costs unless a Viet Cong victory is 100% certain. Never defy Korean soldiers without discrimination, even when are not armed, for they all well trained with Taekwondo.' - An excerpt from an enemy directive seized. - July 22, 1966

[2] A full transcript of the battle of Tra Binh Dong, including how Taekwon-Do was used in it to great effect, can be found in the book *'Ch'ang Hon Taekwon-do Hae Sul'* by the same author.

[3] 'A Savage Week', Time Magazine, 24 February 1967

As General Choi became more and more opposed (and vocal) to President Park's regime he eventually self-exiled himself to Canada in 1972, where he also relocated the ITF headquarters, as well as publishing his third book on Taekwon-Do (known as the Bible of Taekwon-Do). This was the first book to contain all of the 24 patterns of Taekwon-Do.

Taekwon-Do's history is full of politics and it was due to this that the International Taekwon-Do Federation (ITF) headquarters relocated to Canada instead of staying in Korea. It was due to politics that General Choi exiled himself to Canada in 1972 and it was politics that lead to the formation of the World Taekwondo Federation (WTF) in 1973. Sadly, politics has plagued Taekwon-Do all through it short life and continues to do so to this day, even after General Choi passed on the 15th June, 2002.

To read a more in-depth history of Taekwon-Do, please read *'The True And More Complete History Of Taekwon-Do'*, written especially for this book by Taekwon-Do researcher and historian Master George Vitale - it can be found as appendix v, on page 248.

Further to this, if you enjoy learning about the history of Taekwon-Do then I wholeheartedly recommend the following books:

A Killing Art: The Untold History Of Tae Kwon Do
by Alex Gillis

The Korean Martial Art Of Tae Kwon Do & Early History
by Grandmaster Choi, Chang Keun

The Taegeuk Cipher
by Simon John O'Neill

Finally, though I have learned a lot by studying these patterns to ensure they are as correct as possible, I have come to realize just what a momentous task General Choi executed by putting together the original *'Encyclopedia of Taekwon-Do'* as, even with the digital age this was a difficult task, so I can only imagine what it was like in 1983 and just how difficult a task it was with just a 35mm camera and a type writer, even with some of the most gifted and hard-working students (aka the pioneers), the Taekwon-Do world will ever see.

The True History Of The Ch'ang Hon Patterns

The patterns of Ch'ang Hon Taekwon-Do are the signature of the systems creator General Choi Hong Hi. When Taekwon-Do was officially named on 11th April, 1955 not one of the final 24 patterns of Ch'ang Hon Taekwon-do had been finalized, as at this time Taekwon-do still used the Kata from its father art of Shotokan Karate, though this was due to change.

Of course all pattern development was overseen by General Choi himself. He had major technical input into them as well as the final word on them, he was like the director, but other Masters acted out the movements and added their input which helped immensely in their formulation, but they have never received proper credit for it, until now.

(2 Star) General Choi, Hong Hi

Colonel Nam, Tae Hi

A popular misconception is that the patterns were created in order, from *Chon-Ji* onwards, but actually the first official pattern ever devised was *Hwa-Rang*, which was created with the help of Colonel Nam, Tae Hi and Sergeant Han, Cha Kyo in 1955. *Choong-Moo* was the second pattern created in 1955, again with the help of Colonel Nam, Tae Hi, with the third pattern created for the Ch'ang Hon Taekwon-do system being *Ul-Ji* which again, was created with the help of Sergeant Han, Cha Kyo in 1957. Sometime prior to 1958/59 pattern *Sam-Il* was created by General Choi (with the help of the soldiers of the Oh Do Kwan) and it was included in his first book on Taekwon-Do, published in 1959.

It wasn't until 1961 that the next pattern would be finalised. This would be pattern *Ge-Baek* and it was created with the help of Master C.K.Choi, another soldier.

Sergeant Han, Cha Kyo

When General Choi was sent to Malaysia in 1962 fifteen more patterns were created, bringing the total to twenty. It was between 1962 and 1964, with the assistance of his soldiers Master Woo, Jae Lim and Master Kim, Bok Man (who attained the highest non-commissioned officer rank of Sgt. Major) that patterns *Chon-Ji, Dan-Gun, Do-San, Won-Hyo, Yul-Gok, Joong-Gun, Toi-Gye, Kwang-Gae, Po-Eun, Ko-Dang, Choong-Jang, Choi-Yong, Yoo-Sin, Se-Jong* and *Tong-Il* were created, although the actual order is unclear.

Master C.K. Choi

Sometime around 1968 patterns *Eui-Am, Moon-Moo, Yon-Gae* and *So-San* were formulated with the assistance of Master Cho, Sang Min, bringing the final number of patterns to '24', General Choi's ideal number. Master J.C. Kim, Master Park, Jong Soo and Master Lee, Byung Moo among others, may also have helped formulate these patterns.

Master Woo, Jae Lim

Following a trip to North Korea in the early 1980's to secure support for the ITF, pattern *Ko-Dang* was removed and replaced with a new pattern called *Juche*. The reasons for this are discussed all over the internet, as are the merits or demerits of it all. However, whatever ones point of view is, the simple fact remains that it was changed by the founder himself and thus around 1981 pattern *Juche* was created and became an official ITF pattern between 1983 to 1985. It is believed that Master Park, Jung Tae played a major role (if not the major role) in the development of pattern *Juche*, along with assistance form Master Choi, Jung Hwa (General Choi's son), Michael McCormack (General Choi's son-in-law) and Master Lim, Won Sup.

Just prior to this trip, Master Kim, Bok Man, who helped with the formulation of at least 15 patterns in Malaysia between 1962 and 1964 released a book which shows he introduced 4 new patterns for his students called the Silla patterns. These consisted of two empty hand patterns, one knife pattern and a pole pattern. Many believe that Master Kim, Bok Man was opposed to Taekwon-do being a totally empty handed system and wished to have weapons included in its curriculum. The Silla patterns are said to come from the time of the Hwa-rang warriors who existed during the Silla Dynasty in Korea, hence their name.

Master Kim, Bok Man

In 1990 Master Park, Jung Tae parted company with General Choi and the ITF. Up until this point he had been the ITF Secretary-General as well as Chairman of the ITF Instruction Committee, and the man responsible for teaching virtually all Taekwon-do techniques and how they were executed and performed. In 1990 Master Park, Jung Tae formed the Global Taekwon-do Federation (GTF) and further developed six new patterns, often referred to as the *Jee-Goo hyung*. Students within this federation now perform 30 patterns in total including all the original Ch'ang Hon patterns (with *Ko-dang* rather than *Juche*), along with the six new patterns created by Master Park.

Master Cho, Sang Min

As a consequence of Master Park, Jung Tae leaving the ITF the sine-wave motion changed once again. The previous up/down motion was changed to a newer down/up/down motion and later refined to a relax/up/down motion by some organisations, however it is still referred to as *'sine wave'* forcing practioners of the original or older version to rename what they do as *'Natural Motion'*.

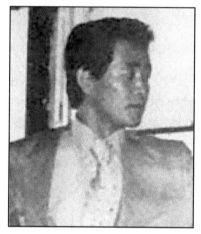

In 2005 the International Ch'ang Hon Taekwon-Do Federation (ICTF) renamed pattern *'Juche'* as *'Ch'ang Hon'* after General Choi's penname and in 2009, the ITF under Grandmaster Choi, Jung Hwa renamed pattern *'Juche'* as *'Ko-Dang'*, however the movements in both cases remain the same as the original pattern *Juche*.

Master J.C. Kim

It should be noted that I have referred to those who helped in the formulation of the Ch'ang Hon patterns by the term Master, when some are now actually Grandmasters. This is not a sign of disrespect for them, but rather a sign of respect for those whose status I do not know.

Though often referred to as the ITF patterns, their correct name is the *Ch'ang Hon* patterns. *Ch'ang Hon* was the pseudonym of General Choi and means *'Blue Cottage'*, so sometimes they are referred to as the *Blue Cottage* patterns or even the *Chon-Ji* patterns, after the first pattern in the set.

Master Park, Jong Soo

Originally they were referred to by their Korean name of *Hyung*, which means *form*, but General Choi later changed this terminology to *tul*, which means *pattern*, as he felt it was a better description of them and was a uniquely Korean term. Master Park, Jung Tae preferred to use the term *hyung*, so when describing his patterns I follow suit, as I have also done with Master Kim, Bok Man's *Silla pattern*, as that was the terminology he chose to use.

Master Lee, Byung Moo

Finally, it is interesting to note that originally, all the patterns were named after famous Korean historical figures or groups, except the first and last ones. The first pattern, '*Chon-Ji*' represents the creation of the world, therefore the creation of Korea as well as the beginning for Taekwon-do students. The last pattern, '*Tong-Ill*' represents the reunification of North and South Korea which was General Choi's lifelong dream; the beginning and the end so to speak. With the change of '*Ko-Dang*' to '*Juche*' however, this changes the equation slightly, but I feel the names of the first and last patterns in the set were highly significant to General Choi and his Korean heritage and ideals.

Master Park, Jung Tae

In an interview conducted in 1999 General Choi was asked how long it took to research his patterns, to which he replied "*I began my research in March 1946 into what was to be named Taekwon-do on April 11, 1955. My research ended in 1983. The patterns represent my study of the Art in this period.*"

Sadly Master Han, Cha Kyo passed in 1996, Master Park, Jung Tae passed away on the 11th April, 2002; 47 years to the day that Taekwon-Do was officially named and General Choi passed away on 15th June 2002. Each has left an enduring mark in Taekwon-do's history and between them they have left their legacy of Taekwon-Do with us.

Differences Between Organisations

Different Taekwon-Do organisations often require their students to perform basic movements in a way that is particular to that organisation. This is mostly due to the time period that the Taekwon-Do organisation base their patterns on i.e. When they separated paths from the ITF or another group, and though there can be minor differences in the way certain techniques are executed, such as aligning a forefist punch with the shoulder, rather than the centre of the body, in the main, these differences are minute and will easily be honed by your own instructor to organisational requirements.

With that said, there are two main areas that do vary from association to association; these are the way blocks are chambered and the way a student moves from one stance to the next and its these differences we detail here. It should be noted that none of them are unequivocally the right way and consequently, none are incorrect either, it is all down to organisational preference.

Chambering Positions When Executing Blocking Techniques

Across the organisations of Taekwon-Do there are 3 main ways that blocks (and some strikes) are chambered. For the examples below we will use the chambering position of a *Left Low Outer Forearm Block*:

A. Wrist to Wrist - A student would align the back of his left wrist, above (or on top) of his left wrist, to the side of his body and execute the block from this position.

B. Forearm to Forearm - A student would align the his left outer forearm above the lower portion of his right outer forearm (sometimes referred to as inside the forearm), to the side of his body and execute the block from this position.

C. Far Back - A student would bring his blocking arm (in this case the left arm) as far back as is possible, bringing it around the body as far as he can reach. For low block this would mean above the shoulder, to the side and execute the block from this position.

Chambering Positions When Executing Striking Techniques

Most organisation execute closed fist striking techniques from similar positions, with minor variations.

Punches are usually executed from the hip, whereas back fists and knifehand strikes are executed from similar positions as blocks; from the side of the body.

Punch and Backfist Chambering Positions

Palm techniques are usually executed from the chest, however some organisations execute them from the hips.

Fingertip thrusts are also mostly executed from chest height, however some organisations execute them from the hips.

Palm and Knifehand Chambering Positions

Straight Fingertip Thrust, Flat Fingertip Thrust and Upset Fingertip Thrust Chambering Positions

Older Straight Fingertip Thrust Chamber Position

In some Taekwon-Do organisations they still use the older chambering motion for a Straight Fingertip Thrust, where the thrusting hand starts from the hip, comes up slightly and shoots forwards (similar to pulling and pointing a pistol from a cowboy style holster).

Knifehands

One quite big difference that needs to be noted relates to knifehands and how they are chambered and travel to their point of impact. Many organisations form the knifehand position from the offset; opened and formed at the chamber position and allow it to travel relaxed but formed to its point of impact. However, some organisations, specifically ITF ones, require the student to chamber a knifehand as a closed fist which travels towards it target relaxed but still closed, only opening into the knifehand at the last possible moment. This applies to both knifehand blocks and knifehand strikes.

Above And Below Show The Two Different Methods Of Executing A Knifehand Strike

Ways Of Moving Between Stances

As with chambering blocks there are various ways of moving from one stance to the next that the various Taekwon-Do organisations require. These are usually related to a specific time period in Taekwon-Do's development and are down to organisational preference. There are 3 main ways of moving:

A. Horizontal Wave - This method sees the student travelling from one stance to the next keeping their head at the same height, with little or no vertical movement. The knees are bent to compensate for the rising of the body as the student moves from one stance to the next. This method is usually utilized by organisations that separated from the ITF in its early years.

B. Natural Motion - This methods sees the students travelling in a natural way from one stance to the next. It allows the natural raising of the body as the student moves forwards before dropping into the technique. This method usually incorporates hip twist as well (see above) and was originally called 'sine-wave' but was changed by some pioneers as a way to distinguish it from the newer version of sine-wave detailed next. This method is usually utilized by organisations that separated from the ITF in the mid 80's or early 90's.

C. Sine-Wave - This method sees the student dropping slightly (or relaxing as some term it) just prior to the start of the movement, then rising as they move forwards before finally dropping into the technique. This method is usually utilized by organisations that remain part of the ITF following the departure of Master Park Jung Tae in the early 90's.

Stepping Between Stances

Like the vertical motions (or lack of) employed when stepping forwards or backwards between stances, the motion the feet travel in also varies and can be separated into 3 distinct methods. In these examples we use the transfer from a left walking stance, stepping forwards into a right walking stance.

A. **In & Out** - This method sees the students right foot travel in so it is next to the left foot, before moving outwards again into the stance.

B. Skating - This method, commonly referred to as *skating* sees the students right foot travel in a small arc as it moves forwards. At a maximum it comes only half a shoulder width in, but usually it is much less than that.

C. Parallel - This method see the student move forwards without moving his foot in at all, as if walking along a set of train tracks.

Spot-Turning / Centre-Line Turns

There are many ways of turning that General Choi employed in the patterns which are referenced in the relevant chapters, however the most common one found is *'Spot -Turning'* (Gujari Dolgi) or as many know it; a *'Centre-Line Turn'* as seen between moves #2 and #3 in Do-San tul and many other places.

Different organisations perform them differently, with some stepping straight across the centre-line and simply turning around (left diagram on page 19), with others moving the front foot 'in' and 'back' before turning and then moving the (now) front foot forwards again (right diagram on page 19). For the sake of uniformity, in these books they are named *'Centre-Line Turns'*.

Methods of Spot Turning/Centre Line Turns

Hip Twist, Sine Wave And Knee-Springs

The two ways that many organisations utilize when striking or blocking are hip twist or sine-wave, with a third way being a combination of the two. These are separate from the *Ways Of Moving Between Stances* as they refer to ways blocks or strikes are executed with or without the forward momentum of moving the whole body. These methods are used when both moving or stationary, with the addition of 'Knee-Spring' that some organisations used for executing techniques stationary, as explained below:

A. Hip Twist - This involves holding the hip back as a student moves or executes a technique before finally flicking it forwards at the last moment to add power into the strike or block. This method is often utilized in conjunction with the horizontal wave (detailed previously). When stationary (as in the pictures above) a student simply withdraws the hip back, then shoots it forwards again as they strike or block.

B. Sine-Wave - A student would drop into a stance to execute a technique and rely solely on the sine-wave relax/up/down motion to add power into the technique without additional hip twist. When stationary (as in the pictures on the previous page) the student simply relaxes, rises and drops again while executing the strike or block. This method is almost specifically used by current ITF students.

C. Combination - The final method is a combination of both the previous methods and utilizes dropping into stance's as well as hip twist to add power. The student would rise naturally as they move or use a knee-spring if stationary (see below), holding the hip back slightly, before flicking it into place as the student drops and executes the technique. This method is most often used in conjunction with the *Natural Motion* way of moving.

Knee-Spring

A knee-spring is utilized by some organisations when executing stationary techniques. It sees the student raising their rear heel and relaxing their rear knee; a slight rising of the body is often seen, as is some hip twist but both are minimal compared to using sine-wave or hip twist alone. As the technique is executed, the rear heel thrusts back to the floor and the rear knee locks straight creating forward power for the block or strike.

How To Use This Book

The main pages of this book are laid out in a specific way in order to transmit as much information as possible to the student. Students have various combinations in the way they like to learn; some can relate straight away to pictures, others like pictures combined with text etc.

Each of the main chapters start with an introduction page, displaying the name of the pattern itself, its standard definition, its diagram and the number of movements it contains.

Nopunde Bakat Palmok Yop Makgi
High Outer Forearm Side Block

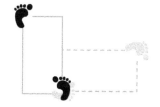

The pages of each patterns chapter (as well as the saju's) displays two or three large numbered pictures of the movement in each patterns sequence. This is combined with various arrows (which are detailed overleaf), which show direction of movement, transition of stances and head (facing) direction amongst other things.

The majority of all the main pictures are shown forward or side facing so techniques can be seen clearly, but where a movement is facing away, a smaller picture appears inset in the main picture to show the correct facing direction it should be executed in. All patterns are shot as if being watched by an examiner.

Underneath the main picture is the terminology of the movement in both Korean and English, and underneath this is a foot diagram showing the previous foot positions as *greyed out* and the new foot positions as black footprints. Below this the movements are described in text form, for example:

32. Pivot on your Right foot 90 degrees anti-clockwise into a *Left Walking Stance*, whilst executing a *High Outer Forearm Side Block* with your left arm.

Finally, at the bottom of each page are a number of small pictures showing how to move from the previous technique to the next, for all the techniques listed on that page. These include the movements in the correct facing direction, as well as chambers and various parts of the transitions from one move to the next.

Previous   *Moves 31, 32 & 33*

The arrows that accompany the main pictures represent the following:

A *large solid arrow* shows the *direction of movement* from one stance to the next in the form of a step (either forwards, backwards or other direction) or a kick.

A *large dashed arrow* shows the *facing direction* following a movement where there is more than just a simple step involved. A *dashed arrow* is used to show that the footwork is more detailed and thus needs to be looked at within the written descriptions. An example of this would be the 2nd movement of Saju Jirugi that has you turning 90 degrees to block, but the foot of the rear leg travels backwards, in the opposite direction to where you are facing. Other examples would be changing from one stance to another without a step forwards, spot-turning/centre-line turns, a step backwards, a spin or a foot shift such as the 2nd and 3rd movements of Won-Hyo tul, where you only shift your front foot forwards from an L-Stance to form a fixed stance.

If there are *no arrows*, then there is no change of stance and no forwards or backwards movement and it is simply an execution of another technique. For example, the Low Block and Rising Block combination in Dan-Gun tul.

Two arrows together show direction of movement while facing another direction, for example, the Back Fist Strike in Toi-Gye tul. The *larger arrow* represents the direction of movement (which may or may not be dashed as detailed above), while the *shorter dashed arrow* represents the way you face upon completion or during execution of the technique.

Finally, a *short dashed arrow* on its own indicates the facing direction of a movement if it changes from the previous movement but doesn't have a step involved. For example, the Low Reverse Knifehand Blocks in Ge-Baek tul, where the stance remains the same, but the facing changes to the opposite side.

Stances and foot positions are represented by footprints upon a rectangle:

The *rectangle* represents the average length and width of a basic Walking Stance, with other stances as slight variations on them. They are incorporated to show how the feet are repositioned in relation to the previous stance of a technique/move. They are used in conjunction with foot prints to show foot placement, with a dashed rectangle with *light foot prints* representing the previous foot positions of the last stance used and *dark foot prints* representing the current foot positions of the new stance or position. The example to the left shows how the student steps from a Right Walking Stance into a Right L-Stance.

ITF Note: .....

On some pages a *boxed piece of text* holds information for students who follow specific systems and holds information pertinent to them, that may be of use as a general note as well. They give information relating to certain sets of movements, for example if combinations are performed in various motions such as Connecting, Continuous, Fast Motion etc.

Finally, at the back of each book are tables relating to pattern orders used by many of the big associations (as they do vary), Kihap points that some organisations use, as well as an in-depth description of various motions and a sine wave study for those that utilise it.

Standards For The Performance Of Patterns

No matter which organisation you practice under, there are a number of standards or rules that are applicable to the way patterns are executed as a solo exercise and include the Saju exercises. These are as follows:

1. **All patterns start and finish on the same spot.**

2. **Each pattern should be performed in a rhythmic motion without stiffness.**

3. **Each technique should be fully formed before moving onto the next.**

4. **Techniques should be performed with realism.**

5. **Correct breathing should be performed throughout each pattern.**

6. **Correct posture and muscle tension should be utilized in all techniques.**

7. **Each pattern should be perfected before moving onto the next.**

Finally, all students of Taekwon-do should remember that *patterns are a series of defensive and offensive movements, set in a logical order against one or more imaginary opponents* and as such, are a core element of Taekwon-Do and its related self defence.

Though there are many benefits to practicing patterns, such as health, flexibility and balance etc., learning them to simply pass a grading or win a medal at a competition is the least important factor of patterns, as without understanding and appreciating them fully, they become little more than a dance routine - and there is so much more to them!

Saju Jirugi
Four Directional Punch

사주 찌르기

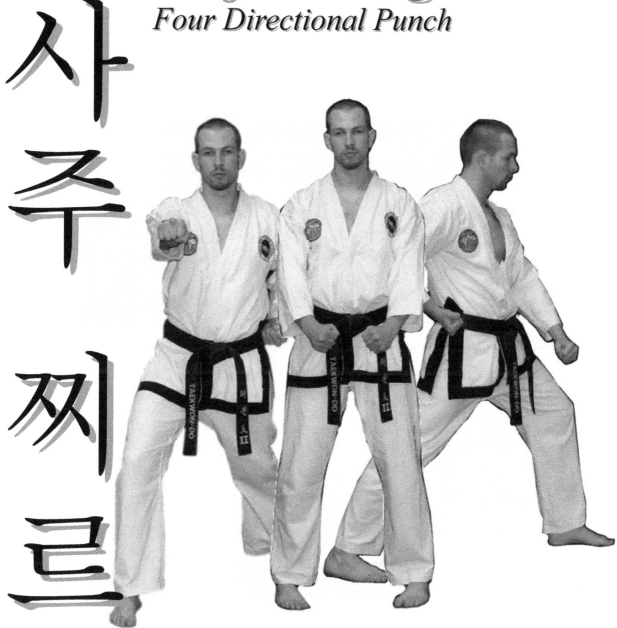

Saju Jirugi is the first of two basic exercises designed to introduce beginning students to various basic elements of Taekwon-do.

Saju Jirugi has 7 movements repeated in both directions

Stepping, Blocking And Punching Motions In Saju Jirugi

Saju Jirugi's diagram is a + shape. The student pivots anti-clockwise following the diagram, with one foot always remaining on the centre mark, before repeating the sequence in the opposite direction.

From a *Right Walking Stance* with *Forefist Punch*, the student moves his lead leg (in this case the right) approximately half way backwards towards his rear leg (left), chambering the *Low Outer Forearm Block* simultaneously, <u>without</u> over-turning his upper body. From this position the student moves his (right) leg backwards into a *Left Walking Stance*, whilst simultaneously turning his body into the block (which is angled when blocking) and executing the *Low Outer Forearm Block*. It is performed in an anti-clockwise direction.

Following the block, the student steps forwards into a *Right Walking Stance* and executes the *Middle Forefist Punch*, before repeating the previous motion. The foot, chambering and pivoting movements are reversed for the opposite side.

Narani Junbi Sogi	**Kaunde Ap**	**Najunde Bakat**
Parallel Ready Stance	**Joomok Jirugi**	**Palmok Makgi**
	Middle Forefist Punch	*Low Outer Forearm Block*

1. From the ready posture (*Parallel Ready Stance)* move forwards into a *Right Walking Stance* and execute a *Middle Forefist Punch* with your Right fist.

2. Bring your Right foot inwards, then pivot 90 degrees anti-clockwise, sliding your Right foot backwards into a *Left Walking Stance* and execute *Low Outer Forearm Block* with your Left arm.

From the Ready Posture to moves 1 & 2

Kaunde Ap Joomok Jirugi
Middle Forefist Punch

Najunde Bakat Palmok Makgi
Low Outer Forearm Block

Kaunde Ap Joomok Jirugi
Middle Forefist Punch

3. Move forwards into a *Right Walking Stance* and execute a *Middle Forefist Punch* with your Right fist.

4. Bring your Right foot inwards, then pivot 90 degrees anti-clockwise, sliding your Right foot backwards into a *Left Walking Stance* and execute *Low Outer Forearm Block* with your Left arm.

5. Move forwards into a *Right Walking Stance* and execute a *Middle Forefist Punch* with your Right fist.

Previous — *Moves 3, 4 & 5*

**Najunde Bakat
Palmok Makgi**
Low Outer Forearm Block

Kaunde Ap Joomok Jirugi
Middle Forefist Punch

6. Bring your Right foot inwards, then pivot 90 degrees anti-clockwise, sliding your Right foot backwards into a *Left Walking Stance* and execute *Low Outer Forearm Block* with your Left arm.

7. Move forwards into a *Right Walking Stance* and execute a *Middle Forefist Punch* with your Right fist.

Previous

Moves 6 & 7

Narani Junbi Sogi
Parallel Ready Stance

Kaunde Ap Joomok Jirugi
Middle Forefist Punch

Najunde Bakat Palmok Makgi
Low Outer Forearm Block

Return. Pivot 90 degrees anti-clockwise, bringing your Right foot forwards into *Parallel Ready Stance*.

1. Move forwards into a *Left Walking Stance* and execute a *Middle Forefist Punch* with your Left fist.

2. Bring your Left foot inwards, then pivot 90 degrees clockwise, sliding your Left foot backwards into a *Right Walking Stance* and execute *Low Outer Forearm Block* with your Right arm .

Previous   *Returning to Parallel Ready Stance and moves 1 & 2*

Kaunde Ap Joomok Jirugi
Middle Forefist Punch

Najunde Bakat Palmok Makgi
Low Outer Forearm Block

Kaunde Ap Joomok Jirugi
Middle Forefist Punch

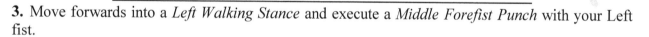

3. Move forwards into a *Left Walking Stance* and execute a *Middle Forefist Punch* with your Left fist.

4. Bring your Left foot inwards, then pivot 90 degrees clockwise, sliding your Left foot backwards into a *Right Walking Stance* and execute *Low Outer Forearm Block* with your Right arm.

5. Move forwards into a *Left Walking Stance* and execute a *Middle Forefist Punch* with your Left fist.

Previous | *Moves 3, 4 & 5*

**Najunde Bakat
Palmok Makgi**
Low Outer Forearm Block

Kaunde Ap Joomok Jirugi
Middle Forefist Punch

6. Bring your Left foot inwards, then pivot 90 degrees clockwise, sliding your Left foot backwards into a *Right Walking Stance* and execute *Low Outer Forearm Block* with your Right arm .

7. Move forwards into a *Left Walking Stance* and execute a *Middle Forefist Punch* with your Left fist. Kihap on last movement.

Previous

Moves 6 & 7

Narani Junbi Sogi
Parallel Ready Stance

Return. Pivot 90 degrees clockwise, bringing your Left foot forwards into *Parallel Ready Stance.*

Previous

Return to the Ready Posture

Tips For Saju Jirugi

1. When pivoting only withdraw the front leg half way in otherwise, when you pivot your next stance can end up too thin.

2. When punching, pull your punch off your hip at the last moment, as you drop into your stance, as opposed to completing your stance then punching.

3. Keep your weight distribution even when performing the low block i.e. Do not lean forwards

4. When chambering to block, do so at the side and ensure, when turning it says at the side and doesn't come to the front allowing the low block to travel on a curve, rather than straight down.

5. Blocks should be completed as the stance is finally formed.

6. Ensure your rear leg is locked on all stances before moving onto the next technique.

Saju Makgi
Four Directional Block

사주 막기

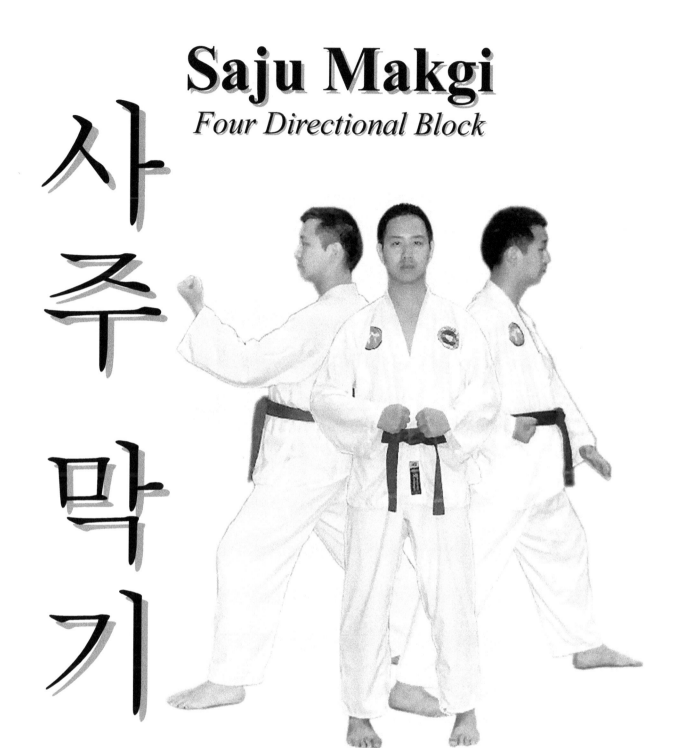

Saju Makgi is the second basic exercise designed to introduce beginning students to various elements of Taekwon-do. Saju Makgi has 8 movements repeated in both directions

Ready Posture

Narani Junbi Sogi
Parallel Ready Stance

#1

Najunde Sonkal Makgi
Low Knifehand Block

#2

Kaunde An Palmok Makgi
Middle Inner Forearm Block

---

1. From the Ready Posture (*Parallel Ready Stance)*, move your Right foot backwards into a *Left Walking Stance* and execute a *Low Knifehand Block* with your Left hand.

2. Move forwards into a *Right Walking Stance* and execute a *Middle Inner Forearm Block* with your Right forearm.

From the ready posture to moves 1, 2, 3 & 4

Najunde Sonkal Makgi
Low Knifehand Block

Kaunde An Palmok Makgi
Middle Inner Forearm Block

Najunde Sonkal Makgi
Low Knifehand Block

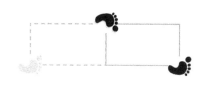

3. Bring your Right foot inwards, then pivot 90 degrees anti-clockwise on your Left foot, sliding your Right foot backwards into a *Left Walking Stance,* executing a *Low Knifehand Block* with your Left hand.

4. Move forwards into a *Right Walking Stance* and execute a *Middle Inner Forearm Block* with your Right forearm.

5. Bring your Right foot inwards, then pivot 90 degrees anti-clockwise on your Left foot, sliding your Right foot backwards into a *Left Walking Stance,* executing a *Low Knifehand Block* with your Left hand.

Chamber position for Low Section Knifehand Block

Chambering for Middle Section Inner Forearm Block

**Kaunde An
Palmok Makgi**
*Middle Inner
Forearm Block*

**Najunde Sonkal
Makgi**
Low Knifehand Block

**Kaunde An
Palmok Makgi**
Middle Inner Forearm Block

6. Move forwards into a *Right Walking Stance* and execute a *Middle Section Inner Forearm Block* with your Right forearm.

7. Bring your Right foot inwards, then pivot 90 degrees anti-clockwise, sliding your Right foot backwards into a *Left Walking Stance,* executing a *Low Knifehand Block* with your Left hand.

8. Move forwards into a *Right Walking Stance* and execute a *Middle Inner Forearm Block* with your Right forearm.

Previous

Moves 5, 6, 7 & 8

Narani Junbi Sogi
Parallel Ready Stance

Najunde Sonkal Makgi
Low Knifehand Block

Kaunde An Palmok Makgi
Middle Inner Forearm Block

Return. Pivot 90 degrees anti-clockwise, bringing your Right foot forwards into *Parallel Ready Stance*.

1. Move your Left leg backwards into a *Right Walking Stance* and execute a *Low Knifehand Block* with your Right hand.

2. Move forwards into a *Left Walking Stance* and execute a *Middle Inner Forearm Block* with your Left arm.

Previous

Moves 1 & 2

39

Najunde Sonkal Makgi
Low Knifehand Block

**Kaunde An
Palmok Makgi**
Middle Inner Forearm Block

**Najunde Sonkal
Makgi**
Low Knifehand Block

3. Bring your Left foot inwards, then pivot 90 degrees clockwise, sliding your Left foot backwards into a *Right Walking Stance,* executing a *Low Knifehand Block* with your Right hand.

4. Move forwards into a *Left Walking Stance* and execute a *Middle Inner Forearm Block* with your Left arm.

5. Bring your Left foot inwards, then pivot 90 degrees clockwise, sliding your Left foot backwards into a *Right Walking Stance,* executing a *Low Knifehand Block* with your Right hand.

Previous   *Moves 3, 4 & 5*

**Kaunde An
Palmok Makgi**
*Middle Inner
Forearm Block*

Najunde Sonkal Makgi
Low Knifehand Block

**Kaunde An
Palmok Makgi**
Middle Inner Forearm Block

6. Move forwards into a *Left Walking Stance* and execute a *Middle Inner Forearm Block* with your Left arm.

7. Bring your Left foot inwards, then pivot 90 degrees clockwise, sliding your Left foot backwards into a *Right Walking Stance,* executing a *Low Knifehand Block* with your Right hand.

8. Move forwards into a *Left Walking Stance* and execute a *Middle Inner Forearm Block* with your Left arm. Kihap on last movement.

Previous

Moves 6, 7 & 8 and return to Ready Posture

Narani Junbi Sogi
Parallel Ready Stance

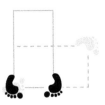

Return. Pivot 90 degrees clockwise, bringing your Left foot forwards into *Parallel Ready Stance*.

Tips For Saju Makgi

1. When pivoting only withdraw the front leg half way in otherwise, when you pivot your next stance can end up too thin.

2. Keep your weight distribution even when performing the low knifehand blocks i.e. Do not lean forwards

3. When chambering to block, do so at the side and ensure, when turning it says at the side and doesn't come to the front allowing the low knifehand block to travel on a curve, rather than straight down.

5. Blocks should be completed as the stance is finally formed.

6. Ensure your rear leg is locked on all stances before moving onto the next technique.

Chon-Ji
Heaven & Earth

천 지 틀

Chon-Ji has 19 movements. Chon-Ji means literally *'the Heaven the Earth'*. It is, in the orient, interpreted as the creation of the world or the beginning of human history, therefore it is the initial pattern played by the beginner. This pattern consists of two similar parts, one to represent the heaven and the other to represent the earth.

Chon-Ji's 90 And 180 Degree Turns

Chon-Ji's is the first official pattern. Like the Saju's, it's diagram is a + shape, however it involves both 90 and 180 degree turns. The first part represents 'heaven', with the block pointing downwards and the second part represents 'earth', with the block pointing upwards.

Chon-Ji has a number of 90 and 180 degree turns into both *Walking Stances* and *L-Stances*. In order to successfully complete the 180 degree turns, the student must step past your centre-line. The dotted line in the pictures travels inline with the left foot in order to show the 'step past centre'. The student turns both clock-wise and anti-clockwise, but its easy to remember which way to turn as the student always turns the side of the previous punch.

In the example above (the first 180 degree turn in Chon-Ji), the student starts off in a *Right Walking Stance* (far right picture). Following the punching arm, the student would pivot just beyond 180 degrees, clockwise, into the next stance (in this case a Right Walking Stance), whilst executing the block. The block chambers as the student is turning and is executed as they complete the next stance. It is exactly the same if going into an L-Stance, with the exception of how you would form the final stance. Below is a 180 degree turn from a *Right Walking Stance* into a *Left L-Stance* (viewed from left to right).

Ready Posture

1

2

Narani Junbi Sogi
Parallel Ready Stance

Najunde Bakat Palmok Makgi
Low Outer Forearm Block

Kaunde Ap Joomok Jirugi
Middle Forefist Punch

---

1. From the ready posture (*Parallel Ready Stance)* step 90 degrees anti-clockwise with your Left foot, forming a *Left Walking Stance* whilst executing a *Low Outer Forearm Block* with your Left arm.

2. Move forwards with your right foot and form a *Right Walking Stance* whilst executing a *Middle Forefist Punch* with your Right fist.

From the Ready Posture to moves 1 & 2

Najunde Bakat Palmok Makgi
Low Outer Forearm Block

Kaunde Ap Joomok Jirugi
Middle Forefist Punch

Najunde Bakat Palmok Makgi
Low Outer Forearm Block

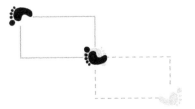

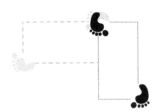

---

3. Pivot 180 degrees clockwise on your Left (rear) foot, forming a *Right Walking Stance* whilst executing a *Low Outer Forearm Block* with your Right arm. This motion is known as '*Backward Step Turning*' (Dwiro Omgyo Didimyo Dolgi).

4. Move forwards with your Left foot and form a *Left Walking Stance* whilst executing a *Middle Forefist Punch* with your Left fist.

5. Pivot 90 degrees anti-clockwise, on your Right (rear) foot, forming a *Left Walking Stance* whilst executing a *Low Outer Forearm Block* with your Left arm.

Moves 3, 4 & 5   *Previous*

Kaunde Ap Joomok Jirugi
Middle Forefist Punch

Najunde Bakat Palmok Makgi
Low Outer Forearm Block

Kaunde Ap Joomok Jirugi
Middle Forefist Punch

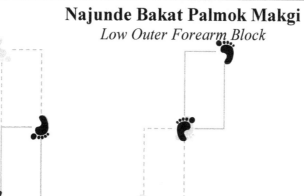

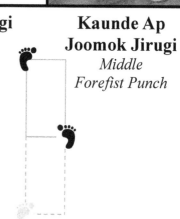

6. Move forwards with your Right foot and form a *Right Walking Stance* whilst executing a *Middle Forefist Punch* with your Right fist.

7. Pivot 180 degrees clockwise on your Left (rear) foot, forming a *Right Walking Stance* whilst executing a *Low Outer Forearm Block* with your Right arm.

8. Move forwards with your Left foot and form a *Left Walking Stance* whilst executing a *Middle Forefist Punch* with your Left fist.

Previous　　　　　*Moves 6, 7 & 8*

Kaunde An Palmok Makgi
Middle Inner Forearm Block

Kaunde Ap Joomok Jirugi
Middle Forefist Punch

9. Pivot 90 degrees anti-clockwise, on your Right (rear) foot, forming a *Right L-Stance* whilst executing a *Middle Inner Forearm Block* with your Left arm.

10. Move forwards with your Right foot and form a *Right Walking Stance* whilst executing a *Middle Forefist Punch* with your Right fist.

Moves 9 & 10   *Previous*

Kaunde An Palmok Makgi
Middle Inner Forearm Block

Kaunde Ap Joomok Jirugi
Middle Forefist Punch

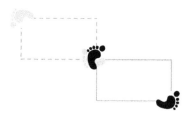

11. Pivot 180 degrees clockwise, on your Left (rear) foot, forming a *Left L-Stance* whilst executing a *Middle Inner Forearm Block* with your Right arm.

12. Move forwards with your Left foot and form a *Left Walking Stance* whilst executing a *Middle Forefist Punch* with your Left fist.

Previous

Moves 11 & 12

Kaunde An Palmok Makgi
Middle Inner Forearm Block

Kaunde Ap Joomok Jirugi
Middle Forefist Punch

Kaunde An Palmok Makgi
Middle Inner Forearm Block

13. Pivot 90 degrees anti-clockwise, on your Right (rear) foot, forming a *Right L-Stance* whilst executing a *Middle Inner Forearm Block* with your Left arm.

14. Move forwards with your Right foot and form a *Right Walking Stance* whilst executing a *Middle Forefist Punch* with your Right fist.

15. Pivot 180 degrees clockwise, on your Left (rear) foot, forming a *Left L-Stance* whilst executing a *Middle Inner Forearm Block* with your Right arm.

Previous   *Moves 13, 14 & 15*

Kaunde Ap Joomok Jirugi
Middle Forefist Punch

Kaunde Ap Joomok Jirugi
Middle Forefist Punch

Kaunde Ap Joomok Jirugi
Middle Forefist Punch

16. Move forwards with your Left foot and form a *Left Walking Stance* whilst executing a *Middle Forefist Punch* with your Left fist.

17. Move forwards with your Right foot and form a *Right Walking Stance* whilst executing a *Middle Forefist Punch* with your Right fist.

18. Move backwards with your Right foot and form a *Left Walking Stance* whilst executing a *Middle Forefist Punch* with your Left fist.

Previous   *Moves 16, 17 & 18*

**Kaunde Ap
Joomok Jirugi**
*Middle
Forefist Punch*

Narani Junbi Sogi
Parallel Ready Stance

19. Move backwards with your Left foot and form a *Right Walking Stance* whilst executing a *Middle Forefist Punch* with your Right fist.

Return. Step your Left foot forwards into *Parallel Ready Stance*.

Previous

Move 19 & return to Ready Posture

Tips For Chon-Ji Tul

1. Ensure you turn and step far enough to form a correct length stance on the first movement; only the rear foot pivots, the left foot steps into the stance.

2. When turning 180 degree's, ensure you step round one stance width past the line of the rear leg, to ensure the stance is the correct width.

3. Chamber blocks as you turn and finalise them as you complete the turn and stance.

4. It is hard to get hip twist into L-Stances, but it can be achieved just a little less than other stances. As you turn, chamber and keep you weight raised before dropping into the stance and completing the technique.

5. Do not rush the last four punches, their rhythm should stay the same as all the techniques in Chon-Ji.

Dan-Gun
Founder Of Korea

Dan-Gun has 21 movements. Dan-Gun is named after the holy Dan-Gun, the legendary founder of Korea in the year 2333 B.C.

Narani Junbi Sogi
Parallel Ready Stance

**Kaunde Sonkal
Daebi Makgi**
Middle Knifehand Guarding Block

Nopunde Ap Joomok Jirugi
High Forefist Punch

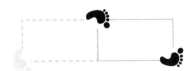

1. From the ready posture (*Parallel Ready Stance)* step 90 degrees to your Left into a *Right L-Stance* and execute a *Middle Section Knifehand Guarding Block*.

2. Move forwards with your Right foot and form a *Right Walking Stance* whilst executing a *High Forefist Punch* with your Right fist.

From the ready posture to moves 1 & 2

**Kaunde Sonkal
Daebi Makgi**
Middle Knifehand Guarding Block

Nopunde Ap Joomok Jirugi
High Forefist Punch

**Najunde Bakat
Palmok Makgi**
*Low Outer
Forearm Block*

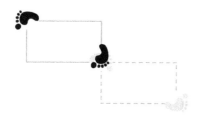

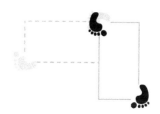

3. Pivot 180 degrees clockwise to form a *Left L-Stance*, whilst executing a *Middle Knifehand Guarding Block*.

4. Move forwards with your Left foot to form a *Left Walking Stance* whilst executing a *High Forefist Punch* with your Left fist.

5. Pivot 90 degrees anti-clockwise on your Right foot, moving your Left foot to form a *Left Walking Stance* whilst executing a *Low Outer Forearm Block* with your Left arm.

Moves 3, 4 & 5

Previous

59

Nopunde Ap Joomok Jirugi
High Forefist Punch

Nopunde Ap Joomok Jirugi
High Forefist Punch

Nopunde Ap Joomok Jirugi
High Forefist Punch

6. Move forwards with your Right foot to form a *Right Walking Stance* whilst executing a *High Forefist Punch* with your Right fist.

7. Move forwards with your Left foot to form a *Left Walking Stance* whilst executing a *High Forefist Punch* with your Left fist.

8. Move forwards with your Right foot to form a *Right Walking Stance* whilst executing a *High Forefist Punch* with your Right fist.

Running from right to left (to show the turn) - Moves 6, 7, 8, 9 & 10   *Previous*

Sang Palmok Makgi
Twin Forearm Block

Nopunde Ap Joomok Jirugi
High Forefist Punch

9. Pivot 90 degrees anti-clockwise on your Right foot to form a *Right L-Stance* whilst executing *Twin Forearm Block*.

10. Move forwards with your Right foot to form a *Right Walking Stance* whilst executing a *High Forefist Punch* with your Right fist.

Reversed view of turning from the Punch into Twin Forearm Block

Sang Palmok Makgi
Twin Forearm Block

Nopunde Ap Joomok Jirugi
High Forefist Punch

**Najunde Bakat
Palmok Makgi**
*Low Outer
Forearm Block*

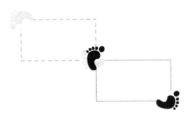

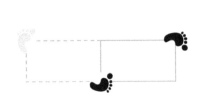

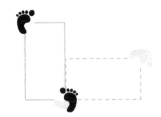

11. Pivot 180 degrees clockwise, on your Left foot to form a *Left L-Stance*, whilst executing a *Twin Forearm Block*.

12. Move forwards with your Left foot to form a *Left Walking Stance* whilst executing a *High Forefist Punch* with your Left fist.

13. Pivot 90 degrees anti-clockwise with your Right foot, moving your Left foot to form a *Left Walking Stance* and execute a *Low Outer Forearm Block* with your Left arm.

Previous

Moves 11, 12, 13 & 14

 # 14

 # 15

 # 16

**Bakat Palmok
Chookyo Makgi**
*Outer Forearm Rising
Block*

**Bakat Palmok
Chookyo Makgi**
*Outer Forearm
Rising Block*

**Bakat Palmok
Chookyo Makgi**
*Outer Forearm
Rising Block*

ITF Note: Movements 13
& 14 are performed in
'Continuous Motion'

14. Maintain your *Left Walking Stance* and execute an *Outer Forearm Rising Block* with your Left arm.

15. Move forwards into a *Right Walking Stance* and execute an *Outer Forearm Rising Block* with your Right arm.

16. Move forwards into a *Left Walking Stance* and execute an *Outer Forearm Rising Block* with your Left arm.

Side view of the turn from move 12 into moves 13 & 14 (showing the combination), followed by stepping in to move 15

**Bakat Palmok
Chookyo Makgi**
*Outer Forearm Rising
Block*

Sonkal Yop Taeragi
Knifehand Side Strike

17. Move forwards into a *Right Walking Stance* and execute an *Outer Forearm Rising Block* with your Right arm.

18. Pivot 90 degrees anti-clockwise on your Right foot, moving your Left foot to form *Right L-Stance* and execute *Knifehand Side Strike* with your Left hand.

Previous · *Moves 15, 16, 17, 18 & 19*

**Nopunde Ap
Joomok Jirugi**
High Forefist Punch

Sonkal Yop Taeragi
Knifehand Side Strike

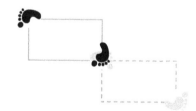

19. Move forwards with your Right foot and form a *Right Walking Stance* whilst executing a *High Forefist Punch* with your Right fist.

20. Pivot 180 degrees clockwise on your Left foot, moving your Right foot to form a *Left L-Stance* and execute *Knifehand Side Strike* with your Right hand.

From right to left - Moves 20 & 21

Previous

Nopunde ApJoomok Jirugi
High Forefist Punch

Narani Junbi Sogi
Parallel Ready Stance

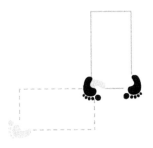

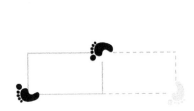

21. Move forwards with your Left foot and form a *Left Walking Stance* whilst executing a *High Forefist Punch* with your Left fist.

Return. Move your Left foot 90 degrees anti-clockwise back into *Parallel Ready Stance*.

Move 21 and return to Ready Posture

Tips For Dan-Gun Tul

1. Chamber the Twin Forearm Blocks as you turn, as opposed to after you turn, then drop into the stance and execute the block in one motion.

2. Do not pre-empt the first rising block. Ensure your Walking Stance is locked straight for the Low Block before executing the Forearm Rising Block.

3. Keep the Knifehand Strike chambered as you turn and strike out at the last second, as opposed to rotating and bringing the Knifehand Strike in a wide arc around the body.

Jee-Sang
On Earth

지 상 형

Jee-Sang means 'On Earth'. This pattern has 24 movements, which symbolize the hours of the day. The diagram represents the four directions: North, South, East and West.

Narani Junbi Sogi
Parallel Ready Stance

Najunde Sonkal Makgi
Low Knifehand Block

Kaunde An Palmok Makgi
Middle Inner Forearm Block

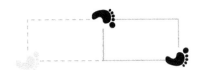

1. From the ready posture (*Parallel Ready Stance*) step 90 degrees to your Left into a *Left Walking Stance* and execute a *Low Knifehand Block* with your Left hand.

2. Move forwards with your Right foot and form a *Right Walking Stance* whilst executing a *Middle Inner Forearm Block* with your Right arm.

From the ready posture to moves 1 & 2

Najunde Sonkal Makgi
Low Knifehand Block

**Kaunde An
Palmok Makgi**
Middle Inner Forearm Block

**Najunde Sonkal
Makgi**
Low Knifehand Block

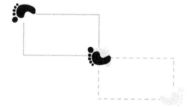

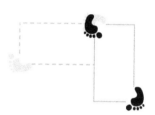

3. Pivot 180 degrees clockwise, moving your Right foot to form a *Right Walking Stance* whilst executing a *Low Knifehand Block* with your Right hand.

4. Move forwards into a *Left Walking Stance* whilst executing a *Middle Inner Forearm Block* with your Left arm.

5. Pivot 90 degrees anti-clockwise moving your Left foot to form a *Left Walking Stance* whilst executing a *Low Knifehand Block* with your Left hand.

Previous

Moves 3, 4 & 5

Kaunde An Palmok Makgi
Middle Inner Forearm Block

Najunde Sonkal Makgi
Low Knifehand Block

Kaunde An Palmok Makgi
Middle Inner Forearm Block

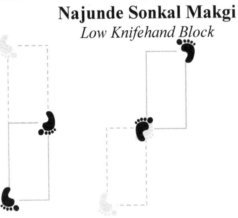

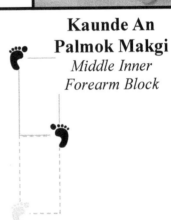

6. Move forwards into a *Right Walking Stance* whilst executing a *Middle Inner Forearm Block* with your Right arm.

7. Pivot 180 degrees clockwise to form a *Right Walking Stance* whilst executing a *Low Knifehand Block* with your Right hand.

8. Move forwards into a *Left Walking Stance* whilst executing a *Middle Inner Forearm Block* with your Left arm.

Previous   *Moves 6, 7 & 8*

Najunde Bakat Palmok Makgi
Low Outer Forearm Block

Kaunde Sonkal Makgi
Middle Knifehand Block

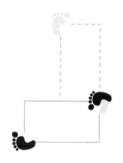

9. Pivot 90 degrees anti-clockwise moving your left foot to form a *Left Walking Stance* whilst executing a *Low Outer Forearm Block* with your Left arm.

10. Move forwards with your Right foot to form a *Left L-Stance* whilst executing a *Middle Knifehand Block* with your Right hand.

Previous

Moves 9 & 10

Najunde Bakat Palmok Makgi
Low Outer Forearm Block

Kaunde Sonkal Makgi
Middle Knifehand Block

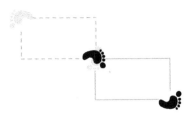

11. Pivot 180 degrees clockwise, moving your Right foot to form a *Right Walking Stance* whilst executing a *Low Outer Forearm Block* with your Right arm.

12. Move forwards with your Left foot to form a *Right L-Stance* whilst executing a *Middle Knifehand Block* with your Left hand.

Previous   *Moves 11 & 12*

Najunde Bakat Palmok Makgi
Low Outer Forearm Block

Kaunde Sonkal Makgi
Middle Knifehand Block

Najunde Bakat Palmok Makgi
Low Outer Forearm Block

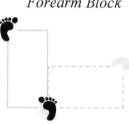

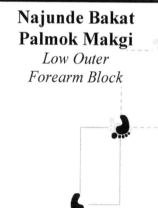

13. Pivot 90 degrees anti-clockwise with your Left foot to form a *Left Walking Stance* and execute a *Low Outer Forearm Block* with your left arm.

14. Move forwards with your Right foot to form a *Left L-Stance* whilst executing a *Middle Knifehand Block* with your Right hand.

15. Pivot 180 degrees clockwise, moving your Right foot to form a *Right Walking Stance* whilst executing a *Low Outer Forearm Block* with your Right arm.

Previous

Moves 13, 14 & 15

Kaunde Sonkal Makgi
Middle Knifehand Block

Ap Cha Olligi
Front Rising Kick

Nopunde An Palmok Yop Makgi
High Inner Forearm Side Block

16. Move forwards with your Left foot to form a *Right L-Stance* whilst executing a *Middle Knifehand Block* with your Left hand.

17. Execute a *Front Rising Kick* with your Right leg.

18. Following the kick, lower your Right foot to form a *Right Walking Stance* while executing a *High Inner Forearm Side Block* with your Right arm.

Previous   *Moves 16, 17 & 18*

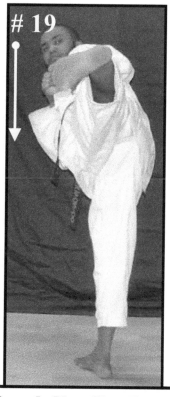

Kaunde Yop Cha Jirugi
Middle Side Piercing Kick

**Nopunde Bandae
Ap Joomok Jirugi**
High Reverse Forefist Punch

Ap Cha Busigi
Front Snap Kick

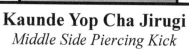

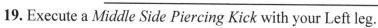

19. Execute a *Middle Side Piercing Kick* with your Left leg.

20. Following the kick, lower your Left foot to form a *Left Walking Stance* while executing a *High Reverse Forefist Punch* with your Right fist.

21. Taking your weight on your Right foot, execute a *Middle Front Snap Kick* with your front (Left) leg.

Previous

Moves 19, 20 & 21

Nopunde Bakat Palmok Yop Makgi
High Outer Forearm Side Block

Kaunde Yop Cha Jirugi
Middle Side Piercing Kick

Nopunde Bandae Ap Joomok Jirugi
High Reverse Forefist Punch

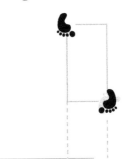

22. Following the kick, lower your Left foot to the rear to form a *Right Walking Stance* while executing a *High Outer Forearm Side Block* with your Right arm.

23. Execute a *Middle Side Piercing Kick* with your front (Right) leg.

24. Following the kick, lower your Right foot to the rear to form a *Left Walking Stance* while executing a *High Reverse Forefist Punch* with your Right fist.

Previous   *Moves 22, 23, 24 & return to ready posture*

Narani Junbi Sogi
Parallel Ready Stance

Return. Move your Left foot backwards into *Parallel Ready Stance*.

Tips For Jee-Sang Hyung

1. Remember that the first 4 (Low) Knifehand Blocks are performed in Walking Stance, while the next 4 (Middle) Knifehand Blocks are performed in L-Stance.

2. Step your foot back, not forwards following the Front Snap Kick (move #21), which comes off the front leg.

3. The 2nd Side Piercing Kick also comes off the front leg, as opposed to the 1st one which comes off the rear leg and you step backwards after executing it.

Do-San

Ahn Chang Ho

도

산

틀

Do-San has 24 movements. Do-San is the pseudonym (pen name) of the patriot Ahn Chang Ho (1878 - 1938*) who devoted his entire life to furthering the education of Korea and its independent movement.

* The countless references to 1876 as Do-Sans birth date are in fact wrong, as Ahn Chang-Ho was actually born in the year 1878 (9ᵗʰ November) and not 1876 according to his own family and historical web site www.ahnchangho.or.kr

Narani Junbi Sogi
Parallel Ready Stance

Nopunde Bakat Palmok Yop Makgi
High Outer Forearm Side Block

Kaunde Bandae Ap Joomok Jirugi
Middle Reverse Forefist Punch

1. From the ready posture (*Parallel Ready Stance)* step 90 degrees to your Left into a *Left Walking Stance* and execute a *High Outer Forearm Side Block* with your Left arm.

2. Maintain your stance and execute a *Middle Reverse Forefist Punch* with your Right fist.

From the ready posture to moves 1 & 2

**Nopunde Bakat Palmok
Yop Makgi**
High Outer Forearm Side Block

**Kaunde Bandae
Ap Joomok Jirugi**
Middle Reverse Forefist Punch

**Kaunde Sonkal
Daebi Makgi**
*Middle Knifehand
Guarding Block*

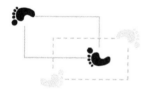

3. Perform a centre-line turn into a *Right Walking Stance* and execute a *High Outer Forearm Side Block* with your Right arm. Centre-Line turns are also known as *Spot Turning* (Gujari Dolgi).

4. Maintain your stance and execute a *Middle Reverse Forefist Punch* with your Left fist.

5. Bring your Left foot half way inwards towards your Right and pivot 90 degrees anti-clockwise on your Right foot, moving your Left foot to form a *Right L-Stance Stance* whilst executing a *Middle Knifehand Guarding Block*.

Previous

Moves 3, 4 & 5

Sun Sonkut Tulgi
Straight Fingertip Thrust

Jappyolsol Tae
Release Move

**Dung Joomok
Nopunde Yop Taeragi**
High Backfist Side Strike

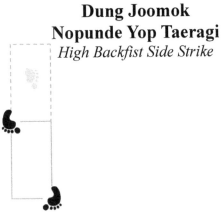

6. Move forwards into a *Right Walking Stance* whilst executing a *Straight Fingertip Thrust* with your Right hand.

6A. Move half a stance inwards with your rear foot while simultaneously twisting your Right hand 180 degrees anti-clockwise and thrusting the whole arm at a downward angle finishing at solar plexus height. *ITF note: Instead of stepping, simply pivot on the balls of your feet and twist your Right hand 90 degrees clockwise.*

7. Following the release above, pivot 180 degrees anti-clockwise into a *Left Walking Stance* and execute a *High Backfist Side Strike* with your Left fist.

Previous

Moves 6 & 7

**Dung Joomok
Nopunde Yop Taeragi**
High Backfist Side Strike

**Nopunde Bakat
Palmok Yop Makgi**
*High Outer Forearm Side
Block*

**Kaunde Bandae Ap
Joomok Jirugi**
Middle Reverse Forefist Punch

8. Move forwards with your Right foot and execute a *High Backfist Side Strike* with your Right fist.

9. Pivot 90 degrees anti-clockwise on your Right foot, moving your Left foot to form a *Left Walking Stance,* executing a *High Outer Forearm Side Block* with your Left arm.

10. Maintain your stance and execute a *Middle Reverse Forefist Punch* with your Right fist.

Previous *Moves 8, 9 & 10*

Nopunde Bakat Palmok Yop Makgi
High Outer Forearm Side Block

**Kaunde Bandae Ap
Joomok Jirugi**
Middle Reverse Forefist Punch

11. Perform a centre-line turn into a *Right Walking Stance* and execute a *High Section Outer Forearm Side Block* with your Right arm.

12. Maintain your stance and execute a *Middle Section Reverse Forefist Punch* with your Left fist.

Previous   *Moves 11 & 12*

Nopunde Bakat Palmok Hechyo Makgi
High Outer Forearm Wedging Block

Ap Cha Busigi
Front Snap Kick

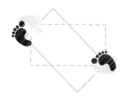

13. Move your Left foot half way towards your Right and pivot 45 degrees on your Right foot and form a *Left Walking Stance* whilst executing a *High Outer Forearm Wedging Block*.

14. Maintain your current angle and execute a *Middle Front Snap Kick* with your Right foot. Keep your arms in the position of the previous Wedging Block as you perform the kick.

Previous

Moves 13 & 14

Kaunde Ap Joomok Jirugi	**Kaunde Bandae Ap Joomok Jirugi**	**Nopunde Bakat Palmok Hechyo Makgi**
Middle Forefist Punch	*Middle Reverse Forefist Punch*	*High Outer Forearm Wedging Block*

ITF Note: Movements 15 & 16 are performed in *'Fast Motion'*

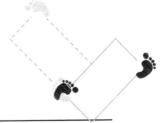

15. Land (from the kick) into a *Right Walking Stance*, executing a *Right Forefist Punch* as you land.

16. Maintain your stance and execute a *Reverse Forefist Punch* with your Left fist.

17. Move your Right foot backwards (approximately half way) before pivoting 90 degrees clockwise on your Left foot, moving your Right foot forwards to form a *Right Walking Stance* whilst executing a *High Outer Forearm Wedging Block*.

Previous   *Moves 15, 16 & 17*

88

Ap Cha Busigi
Front Snap Kick

Kaunde Ap Joomok Jirugi
Middle Forefist Punch

Kaunde Bandae Ap Joomok Jirugi
Middle Reverse Forefist Punch

ITF Note: Movements 19 & 20 are performed in *'Fast Motion'*

18. Maintain your current angle, execute a *Middle Front Snap Kick* with your Left foot. Keep your arms in the position of the previous Wedging Block as you perform the kick.

19. Land (from the kick) into a *Left Walking Stance*, executing a *Left Forefist Punch* as you land.

20. Maintain your stance and execute a *Reverse Forefist Punch* with your Right fist.

Previous

Moves 18, 19 & 20

21

Bakat Palmok Chookyo Makgi
Outer Forearm Rising Block

22

Bakat Palmok Chookyo Makgi
Outer Forearm Rising Block

23

Kaunde Sonkal Yop Taeragi
Middle Knifehand Side Strike

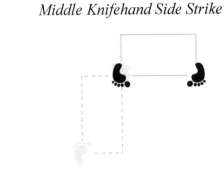

21. Pivot on your Right foot - moving your Left foot so you straighten up towards the start position, and form *a Left Walking Stance* whilst executing an *Outer Forearm Rising Block* with your Left arm.

22. Move forward into a *Right Walking Stance* and execute an *Outer Forearm Rising Block* with your Right arm.

23. Pivot 90 degrees anti-clockwise on your Right foot, moving your Left foot to form a *Sitting Stance* whilst executing a *Middle Knifehand Side Strike* with your Left hand.

Previous

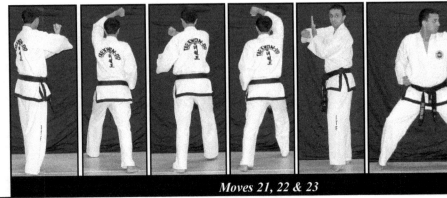

Moves 21, 22 & 23

Kaunde Sonkal Yop Taeragi
Middle Knifehand Side Strike

Narani Junbi Sogi
Parallel Ready Stance

24. Move your Left foot in towards your right foot (foot to foot), then step your Right foot out to the Right (chambering the Knifehand as you move) to form a Sitting Stance whilst executing a *Middle Knifehand Side Strike* with your Right hand.

Return. Move your Right foot back into *Parallel Ready Stance*.

Previous

Move 24 & return to Ready Stance

Tips For Do-San Tul

1. When performing a centre-line turn (also known as 'spot turning') ensure you bring your front foot back about 3 inches to the centre-line (running through the middle of your stance), then pivot on the ball of the same foot, turning 180 degrees before moving the other foot forwards, as this creates forward momentum.

2. Do not pre-empt the Release Technique that follows the Straight Fingertip Thrust, ensure your Walking Stance is fully locked before continuing on.

3. Following the Release Technique as you rotate round, be sure to keep your left fist underneath your arm until you unload the Back Fist Strike. A common mistake is to let it slip out and end up delivering it from above the reaction arm.

4. Wedging Blocks should rise up centrally as you move into your stance, coming up higher than the finishing height of the block. The block finishes by pulling the arms downwards and outwards as you finish your stance.

5. Be sure to keep Wedging Blocks a shoulder width only. A common error is to allow them to go too wide.

6. When performing Double Punches, in this case following the Front Snap kick, the first of the punches is executed as you drop into your stance, not afterwards.

7. When stepping between the final two Sitting Stances, rise up as you step foot to foot but do not lock your legs straight.

Won-Hyo
Noted Monk

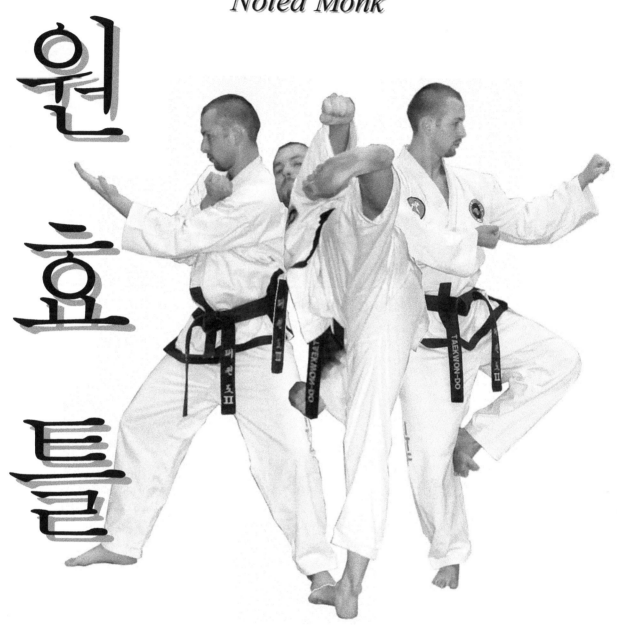

Won-Hyo has 28 movements. Won-Hyo was a noted monk who introduced Buddhism to the Silla dynasty in the year 686 AD.

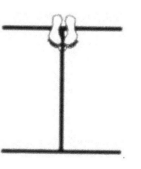

Moa Junbi Sogi 'A'
Closed Ready Stance 'A'

Sang Palmok Makgi
Twin Forearm Block

**Sonkal Nopunde
Anuro Taeragi**
Knifehand High Inward Strike

Note: The direct translation of *'Moa'* is actually *'Close'*, but most use the terminology *'Closed'*, so I have stayed with the most common term used throughout this book.

ITF Note: ITF students no longer perform the grabbing motion between moves 1 & 2 or 4 & 5

Pre. From the pre-ready posture, raise up on your Right foot slightly, bringing your Left foot in to your right (off the ground), whilst simultaneously bringing your hands to the ready posture position.

1. From *Closed Ready Stance 'A'*, step 90 degrees to your Left and form a *Right L-Stance* whilst executing a *Twin Forearm Block.*

2. Maintain your stance and execute a *Knifehand High Inward Strike* with your Right hand, pulling Left fist to Right shoulder. Rise and drop into the stance without moving your feet.

Pre-ready position

From the ready posture to moves 1 & 2

Gojang Sogi,
Kaunde Ap Joomok Jirugi
Fixed Stance, Middle Forefist Punch

Sang Palmok Makgi
Twin Forearm Block

3. Pull Left foot half way towards Right foot, then move it forwards into a *Left Fixed Stance* and execute a *Middle Forefist Punch* with your Left fist.

4. Move Left foot to Right foot then move in the opposite direction (your Right) and form a *Left L-Stance* whilst executing a *Twin Forearm Block*.

Previous   *Moves 3 & 4*

**Sonkal Nopunde
Anuro Taeragi**
Knifehand High Inward Strike

**Gojang Sogi,
Kaunde Ap Joomok Jirugi**
Fixed Stance, Middle Forefist Punch

5. Maintain your stance and execute a *Knifehand High Inward Strike* with your Left hand, pulling Right fist to Left shoulder. Rise and drop into the stance without moving feet.

6. Pull Right foot half way towards Left foot, then move it forwards into a *Right Fixed Stance* and execute a *Middle Forefist Punch* with your Right fist.

Moves 5 & 6

Previous

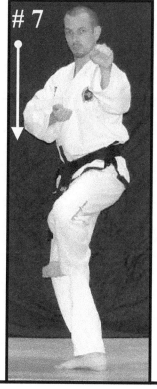

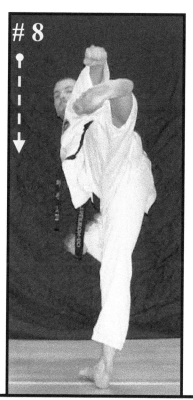

Goburyo Junbi Sogi 'A'
Bending Ready Stance 'A'

Kaunde Yop Cha Jirugi
Middle Side Piercing Kick

Kaunde Sonkal Daebi Makgi
Middle Knifehand Guarding Block

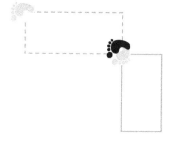

7. Bring your Right foot in to your Left, turn 90 degrees anti-clockwise and perform a *Right Bending Ready Stance 'A'*. Bend your rear leg slightly as you execute the stance.

8. From the Bending Ready Stance, without dropping your leg, chamber and execute a *Left Middle Side Piercing Kick*.

9. Following the Side Piercing Kick, land in a *Right L-Stance* and execute a *Middle Knifehand Guarding Block*.

Previous

Moves 7, 8 & 9

Kaunde Sonkal Daebi Makgi
Middle Knifehand Guarding Block

Kaunde Sonkal Daebi Makgi
Middle Knifehand Guarding Block

Sun Sonkut Tulgi
Straight Fingertip Thrust

10. Move forwards into a *Left L-Stance* and execute a *Middle Knifehand Guarding Block*.

11. Move forwards into a *Right L-Stance* and execute a *Middle Knifehand Guarding Block*.

12. Move forwards into a *Right Walking Stance* whilst executing a *Straight Fingertip Thrust* with the Right hand, placing Left hand (fingertips) under your Right elbow.

Performing Bending Ready Stance, Side Piercing Kick & landing in Kinfehand Guarding Block

Sang Palmok Makgi
Twin Forearm Block

**Sonkal Nopunde
Anuro Taeragi**
Knifehand High Inward Strike

13. Pivot 90 degrees anti-clockwise on your Right foot and form a *Right L-Stance* while executing a *Twin Forearm Block*.

14. Maintain your stance and execute a *Knifehand High Inward Strike* with your Right hand, pulling Left fist to Right shoulder. Rise and drop into the stance without moving your feet.

Previous   *Moves 10, 11, 12, 13 & 14*

**Gojang Sogi,
Kaunde Ap Joomok Jirugi**
Fixed Stance, Middle Forefist Punch

Sang Palmok Makgi
Twin Forearm Block

15. Pull Left foot half way towards Right foot, then move it forwards into a *Left Fixed Stance* and execute a *Middle Forefist Punch* with your Left fist.

16. Move Left foot to Right foot and step the opposite direction (your right) and form a *Left L-Stance* whilst executing a *Twin Forearm Block*.

Previous

Moves 15 & 16

**Sonkal Nopunde
Anuro Taeragi**
Knife-hand High Inward Strike

**Gojang Sogi,
Kaunde Ap Joomok Jirugi**
Fixed Stance, Middle Forefist Punch

17. Maintain your stance and execute a *Knifehand High Inward Strike* with your Left hand, pulling right fist to Left shoulder. Rise and drop into the stance without moving feet.

18. Pull Right foot half way towards Left foot, then move it forwards into a *Right Fixed Stance* and execute a *Middle Forefist Punch* with your Right fist.

Previous

Moves 17 & 18

Dollimyo Makgi
Circular Block

Najunde Ap Cha Busigi
Low Front Snap Kick

**Kaunde Bandae Ap
Joomok Jirugi**
*Middle Reverse
Forefist Punch*

19. Move your Right foot to your Left foot (foot to foot) and turn 90 degrees anti-clockwise, then step your Left leg forwards into a *Left Walking Stance* and execute a *Right Circular Block*.

20. Execute a *Low Front Snap Kick* with your Right leg, maintaining the previous hand position.

21. Following the Front Snap Kick, land in a *Right Walking Stance*, simultaneously executing a *Left Reverse Punch*.

Previous   *Moves 19, 20 & 21*

Dollimyo Makgi
Circular Block

Najunde Ap Cha Busigi
Low Front Snap Kick

**Kaunde Bandae
Ap Joomok Jirugi**
*Middle Reverse
Forefist Punch*

22. Maintain your stance and execute a *Left Circular Block*.

23. Execute a *Low Front Snap Kick* with your Left leg, maintaining the previous hand position.

24. Following the Front Snap Kick, land in a *Left Walking Stance*, simultaneously executing a *Right Reverse Punch*.

Performing Circular Block

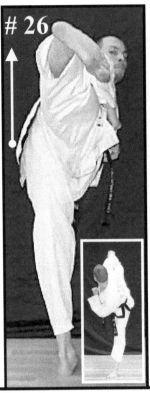

Goburyo Junbi Sogi 'A'
Bending Ready Stance 'A'

Kaunde Yop Cha Jirugi
Middle Side Piercing Kick

**Kaunde Palmok
Daebi Makgi**
Middle Forearm Guarding Block

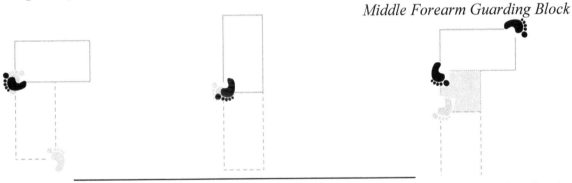

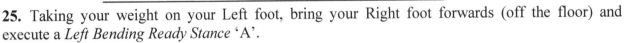

25. Taking your weight on your Left foot, bring your Right foot forwards (off the floor) and execute a *Left Bending Ready Stance* 'A'.

26. From the Bending Ready Stance, without dropping your leg, chamber and execute a *Right Middle Side Piercing Kick*.

27. Following the Side Piercing Kick, land your Right foot approximately one shoulder width from your Left foot (on your start position), then pivot 90 degrees anti-clockwise on your Right foot to form a *Right L-Stance* while executing a *Middle Forearm Guarding Block*.

Previous   *Moves 22, 23, 24, 25, 26 & 27*

Kaunde Palmok
Daebi Makgi
Middle Forearm Guarding
Block

Moa Junbi Sogi 'A'
Closed Ready Stance 'A'

28. Move foot to foot (Left to Right), then move into a *Left L-Stance* and execute a *Middle Forearm Guarding Block.*

Return. Bring your Right foot back to *Closed Ready Stance 'A' (*the Ready Posture).

Previous   *Move 28 (finish) & return to Ready Stance*

Tips For Won-Hyo Tul

1. Do not move your feet when performing the first two moves of the first and second combinations, simply rise and drop into the 2nd stance. It is only on the 3rd and 6th technique that the foot is moved. The same applies when repeating them again within the pattern.

2. A common error is to punch from the chest following the Knifehand Strikes, so be sure to pull the fist to your hip first.

3. Bend your supporting leg when executing a Bending Ready Stance, as this will aid balance.

4. Circular Block should be performed in a smooth motion with no stop, though it is useful to consider two targets; one low and one middle when executing it.

5. When performing a Circular Block do not lean forwards into it, instead bend both knees to lower your height, locking the rear leg back into place following the block. This will allow you to keep your body straight.

Dhan-Goon
Founder Of Korea

단 군 형

Dhan-Goon was created after the holy Dan-Gun, the legendary founder of Korea in the year 2333 B.C. Dhan-Goon has 23 movements which stand for the first two digits of the year 2333 B.C.

Narani Junbi Sogi
Parallel Ready Stance

Kaunde An Palmok Makgi
Middle Inner Forearm Block

1. From *Parallel Ready Stance*, step 90 degrees to your Left and form a *Right L-Stance* whilst executing a *Middle Inner Forearm Block*.

From the ready posture to moves 1

Kaunde Ap Joomok Jirugi
Middle Forefist Punch

Kaunde An Palmok Makgi
Middle Inner Forearm Block

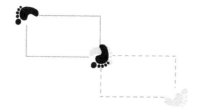

2. Move forwards to form a *Right Walking Stance* while executing a *Right Middle Forefist Punch*.

3. Moving your Right foot clockwise, pivot 180 degrees to form a *Left L-Stance* while executing a *Middle Inner Forearm Block*.

Previous

Moves 2 & 3

Kaunde Ap Joomok Jirugi
Middle Forefist Punch

Najunde Bakat Palmok Makgi
Low Outer Forearm Block

Kaunde Ap Cha Busigi
Middle Front Snap Kick

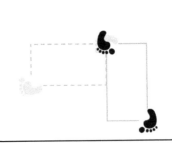

4. Move forwards to form a *Left Walking Stance* while executing a *Left Middle Forefist Punch*.

5. Move your Left foot 90 degrees anti-clockwise to form a *Left Walking Stance* and execute a *Low Outer Forearm Block* with your Left arm.

6. Execute a *Middle Front Snap Kick* with your Right leg.

Previous   *Moves 4, 5 & 6*

**Kaunde Ap
Cha Busigi**
Middle Front Snap Kick

Kaunde Yop Cha Jirugi
Middle Side Piercing Kick

Sonkal Yop Taeragi
Knifehand Side Strike

7. Following the kick, lower your Right foot in front and execute a *Middle Front Snap Kick* with your Left leg.

8. Following the kick, lower your Left foot in front and execute a *Middle Side Piercing Kick* with your Right leg.

9. Following the Side Piercing Kick, lower your Right foot in front forming a *Left L-Stance* and execute a *Middle Knifehand Side Strike* with your Right hand.

Previous

Moves 7, 8 & 9

Kaunde Sonkal Daebi Makgi
Middle Knifehand Guarding Block

Kaunde Ap Joomok Jirugi
Middle Forefist Punch

10. Moving your Left foot, pivot 90 degrees anti-clockwise to form a *Right L-Stance* while executing a *Middle Knifehand Guarding Block*.

11. Move forwards into a *Right Walking Stance* and execute a *Middle Forefist Punch* with your Right hand.

Previous   *Moves 10 & 11*

Kaunde Sonkal Daebi Makgi
Middle Knifehand Guarding Block

Kaunde Ap Joomok Jirugi
Middle Forefist Punch

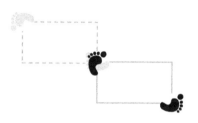

12. Moving your Right foot, pivot 180 degrees clockwise to form a *Left L-Stance* while executing a *Middle Knifehand Guarding Block*.

13. Move forwards into a *Left Walking Stance* and execute a *Middle Forefist Punch* with your Left hand.

Previous

Moves 12 & 13

Nopunde An Palmok Yop Makgi
High Inner Forearm Side Block

Nopunde Bandae Ap Joomok Jirugi
High Reverse Forefist Punch

Sang Palmok Makgi
Twin Forearm Block

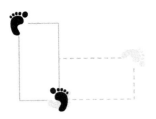

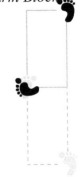

14a. Move your Left foot 90 degrees anti-clockwise to form a *Left Walking Stance* while executing a *High Inner Forearm Side Block* with your Left arm.

14b. Maintain your stance and execute a *High Reverse Forefist* Punch with your Right fist.

15a. Move your Right foot forwards to form a *Left L-Stance* while executing a *Twin Forearm Block*.

Previous   *Moves 14a, 14b & 15a*

**Nopunde Dollyo
Goro Chagi**
High Hooking Kick

**Nopunde Bandae
Ap Joomok Jirugi**
High Reverse Forefist Punch

Goburyo Junbi Sogi 'A'
Bending Ready Stance 'A'

15b. Taking your weight on your Left foot, execute a *High Hooking Kick* with your front (Right) leg.

15c. Following the kick, lower your Right foot to form a *Right Walking Stance* while executing a *High Reverse Forefist* Punch with your Left fist.

16. Bring your Left foot forwards and form a *Right Bending Ready Stance 'A'*.

Previous — *Moves 15b, 15c & 16*

Kaunde Yop Cha Jirugi
Middle Side Piercing Kick

Kaunde Palmok Daebi Makgi
Middle Forearm Guarding Block

17. Without putting your foot down, execute a *Middle Side Piercing Kick* with your Left leg.

18. Following the Side Piercing Kick, lower your Left foot to your start position, before pivoting 90 degrees clockwise (moving your Right foot) to form a *Left L-Stance* and executing a *Middle Forearm Guarding Block*.

Previous   *Moves 17 & 18*

Nopunde Dollyo Chagi
High Turning Kick

**Nopunde Bandae
Ap Joomok Jirugi**
High Reverse Forefist Punch

19. Execute a *High Turning Kick* with your Left leg.

20. Following the kick, lower your Left foot in front to form a *Left Walking Stance* while executing *High Reverse Forefist Punch* with your Right fist.

Previous   *Moves 19 & 20*

Kaunde Palmok Daebi Makgi
Middle Forearm Guarding Block

Nopunde Dollyo Chagi
High Turning Kick

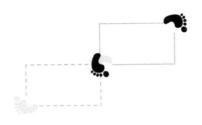

21. Moving your Left foot, pivot 180 degrees anti-clockwise to form a *Right L-Stance* while executing a *Middle Forearm Guarding Block*.

22. Execute a *High Turning Kick* with your Right leg.

Previous   *Moves 21 & 22*

**Nopunde Bandae
Ap Joomok Jirugi**
High Reverse Forefist Punch

Narani Junbi Sogi
Parallel Ready Stance

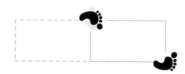

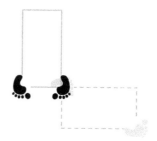

---

23. Following the kick, lower your Right foot in front to form a *Right Walking Stance* while executing *High Reverse Forefist Punch* with your Left fist.

Return. Bring your right foot back to *Parallel Ready Stance* (the Ready Posture).

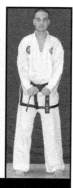

Previous

Move 23 & return to ready posture

Tips For Dhan-Goon Hyung

1. Dhan-Goon Hyung seems a fairly straight forward pattern until you come to move #15b (The High Hooking Kick) which is a difficult technique for this level. Practice the High Hooking Kick separately from the pattern to improve it.

Yul-Gok

Confucius Of Korea

Yul-Gok is the pseudonym of a great philosopher and scholar Yi I, nicknamed the Confucius of Korea (1536-1584). Yul-Gok has 38 movements which represent his birth place on 38 degrees latitude and the diagram represents scholar.

Narani Junbi Sogi
Parallel Ready Stance

Annun Sogi
Sitting Stance (extend fist)
(slow motion)

Note: On move 1, Some extend the fist in a slow motion punch, whilst others (ITF) raise it straight up

1. From *Narani Junbi Sogi*, step to your Left into a *Sitting Stance*, whilst extending your Left fist. Perform in slow motion.

From the Ready Posture to moves 1, 2 & 3

Kaunde Ap Joomok Jirugi
Middle Forefist Punch

Kaunde Ap Joomok Jirugi
Middle Forefist Punch

ITF Note: Movements 2 & 3 are performed in *'Fast Motion'*

2. Maintain your stance and execute a *Middle Forefist Punch* with your Right fist.

3. Maintain your stance and execute a *Middle Forefist Punch* with your Left fist.

Annun Sogi
Sitting Stance (extend fist)
(slow motion)

Kaunde Ap Joomok Jirugi
Middle Forefist Punch

Note: On move 4, some organisations extend the fist in a slow motion punch, whilst other ITF/ITF affiliated organisations raise it straight up

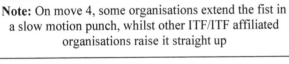

4. Move foot to foot (Left to Right) into a *Sitting Stance* whilst extending your Left fist. Perform in slow motion.

5. Maintain your stance and execute a *Middle Forefist Punch* with your Left fist.

Moves 4, 5 & 6   *Previous*

Kaunde Ap Joomok Jirugi
Middle Forefist Punch

ITF Note: Movements 5 & 6 are performed in 'Fast Motion'

Nopunde An Palmok Makgi
High Inner Forearm Block

ITF Note: Move 7 is now Middle

6. Maintain your stance and execute a *Middle Forefist Punch* with your Right fist.

7. Pivot 30 degrees clockwise on your Left foot to form a *Right Walking Stance,* executing a *High Inner Forearm Block* with your Right arm.

Move 7

Previous

Najunde Ap Cha Busigi
Low Front Snap Kick

**Kaunde Ap
Joomok Jirugi**
Middle Forefist Punch

**Kaunde Bandae Ap
Joomok Jirugi**
Middle Reverse Forefist Punch

> **ITF Note:** Movements 9 & 10 are performed in *'Fast Motion'*

8. Maintain your current direction and execute a *Low Front Snap Kick* with your Left leg. Keep your arms in the previous block position.

9. Upon landing execute a *Middle Obverse Punch* as you drop into a *Left Walking Stance*.

10. Maintain your stance and execute a *Reverse Forefist Punch* with your Right fist.

Moves 8, 9 & 10

Previous

Nopunde An Palmok Makgi
High Inner Forearm Block

ITF Note: Move 11 is now Middle

Najunde Ap Cha Busigi
Low Front Snap Kick

Kaunde Ap Joomok Jirugi
Middle Forefist Punch

11. Pivot 60 degrees anti-clockwise to form a *Left Walking Stance* and execute a *High Inner Forearm Block* with your Left arm.

12. Maintain your current direction and execute a *Low Front Snap Kick* with your Right leg. Keep your arms in the previous block position.

13. Upon landing execute a *Middle Obverse Punch* as you drop into a *Right Walking Stance*.

Previous   *Moves 11, 12 13 & 14*

**Kaunde Bandae Ap
Joomok Jirugi**
Middle Reverse Forefist Punch

**Kaunde Sonbadak
Golcha Makgi**
Middle Palm Hooking Block

**Kaunde Sonbadak
Golcha Makgi**
Middle Palm Hooking Block

ITF Note: Movements 13 & 14 are performed in 'Fast Motion'

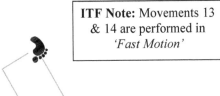

14. Maintain your stance and execute a *Reverse Forefist Punch* with your Left fist.

15. Pull your Right foot in slightly and straighten up by moving it 30 degrees clockwise to form a *Right Walking Stance* and execute a *Palm Hooking Block* with your Right palm.

16. Maintain your stance and execute a *Palm Hooking Block* with your Left palm.

Previous

Moves 15, 16 & 17

**Kaunde Ap
Joomok Jirugi**
Middle Forefist Punch

ITF Note: Movements 16 & 17 are
performed in *'Connecting Motion'*

**Kaunde Sonbadak
Golcha Makgi**
*Middle Palm Hooking
Block*

**Kaunde Sonbadak
Golcha Makgi**
*Middle Palm Hooking
Block*

17. Maintain your stance and execute a *Middle Obverse Punch* with your Right fist.

18. Move forwards into a *Left Walking Stance* and execute a *Palm Hooking Block* with your Left palm.

19. Maintain your stance and execute a *Palm Hooking Block* with your Right palm.

Side view of performing the Palm Hooking Block combination from the Reverse Punch (moves 14, 15 & 16)

**Kaunde Ap
Joomok Jirugi**
Middle Forefist Punch

**Kaunde Ap
Joomok Jirugi**
Middle Forefist Punch

**Goburyo Junbi
Sogi 'A'**
Bending Ready

ITF Note: Movements 19 & 20 are performed in *'Connecting Motion'*

20. Maintain your stance and execute a *Middle Obverse Punch* with your Left fist.

21. Move forwards into a *Right Walking Stance* and execute a *Middle Obverse Punch* with your Right fist.

22. Bring your Left leg forwards and form a *Right Bending Ready Stance 'A'*.

Previous   *Moves 18, 19, 20, 21 & 22*

Kaunde Yop Cha Jirugi
Middle Side Piercing Kick

Ap Palkup Taeragi
Front Elbow Strike

Goburyo Junbi Sogi 'A'
Bending Ready Stance 'A'

23. From the Bending Ready Stance, execute a *Middle Side Piercing Kick* with your Left leg.

24. Following the Side Piercing Kick, land in a *Left Walking Stance* and execute a *Right Front Elbow Strike* to your Left palm.

25. Without stepping, immediately pivot 180 degrees on your Left leg and execute a *Left Bending Ready Stance 'A'* .

*Side view of the Side Piercing Kick, Front Elbow Strike &
turn into the next stance*

Previous   Moves 22, 23, 24 & 25

Kaunde Yop Cha Jirugi
Middle Side Piercing Kick

Ap Palkup Taeragi
Front Elbow Strike

Sang Sonkal Makgi
Twin Knifehand Block

26. From the Bending Ready Stance, without dropping your leg, chamber and execute a *Right Middle Side Piercing Kick*.

27. Following the Side Piercing Kick, land in a *Right Walking Stance* and execute a *Left Front Elbow Strike* to your Right palm.

28. Slip your Left foot inwards to yours Right foot and pivot 90 degrees anti-clockwise, slipping the Left foot outwards again to form a *Right L-Stance*, whilst executing a *Twin Knifehand Block*.

Previous — *Moves 26, 27 & 28 plus reversed view of chambering move 28*

Sun Sonkut Tulgi
Straight Fingertip Thrust

Sang Sonkal Makgi
Twin Knifehand Block

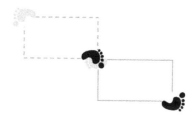

29. Move forwards to form a *Right Walking Stance* and execute a *Straight Fingertip Thrust* with your Right hand.

30. Pivot 180 degrees clockwise on your Left (rear) foot, moving your Right foot to form a *Left L-Stance*, whilst executing a *Twin Knifehand Block*.

Previous

Moves 29 & 30

Sun Sonkut Tulgi
Straight Fingertip Thrust

Nopunde Bakat Palmok Yop Makgi
High Outer Forearm Side Block

Kaunde Bandae Ap Joomok Jirugi
Middle Reverse Forefist Punch

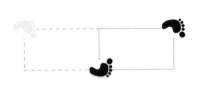

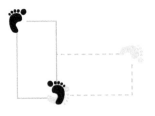

31. Move forwards to form a *Left Walking Stance* and execute a *Straight Fingertip Thrust* with your Left hand.

32. Move your Left foot 90 degrees anti-clockwise into a *Left Walking Stance*, whilst executing a *High Outer Forearm Side Block* with your Left arm.

33. Maintain your stance and execute a *Middle Reverse Forefist Punch* with your Right fist.

Previous

Moves 31, 32 & 33

34

35

36

Nopunde Bakat Palmok Yop Makgi
High Outer Forearm Side Block

Kaunde Bandae Ap Joomok Jirugi
Middle Reverse Forefist Punch

Kyocha Sogi, Nopunde Dung Joomok Taeragi
X-Stance, High Back Fist Strike

34. Move forwards into a *Right Walking Stance*, whilst executing a *High Outer Forearm Side Block* with your Right arm.

35. Maintain your stance and execute a *Middle Reverse Forefist Punch* with your Left fist.

36. Bring your Left (rear) foot forwards and past your right in a *'striding'* motion and jump approximately 1 stance length, forming a *Left X-Stance*, whilst executing a *Left High Backfist Strike*. The jump is performed to gain distance, not height.

Previous | *Moves 34, 35 & 36*

Nopunde Doo Palmok Makgi

High Double Forearm Block

Nopunde Doo Palmok Makgi

High Double Forearm Block

Narani Junbi Sogi

Parallel Ready Stance

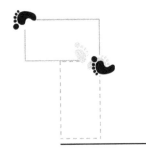

37. Pivot 270 degrees clockwise on your Left foot, moving your Right foot to form a *Right Walking Stance* and execute a *High Double Forearm Block*.

38. Move foot to foot (Right foot to Left) and pivot 180 degrees anti-clockwise, stepping into a *Left Walking Stance* whilst executing a *High Double Forearm Block*.

Return. Bring your Left foot back to *Narani Junbi Sogi (the Ready Posture)*.

Previous | *Move 37, 38 & return to Ready Posture*

Yul-Gok Extras

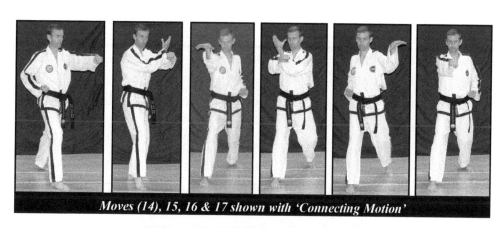

Moves (14), 15, 16 & 17 shown with 'Connecting Motion'

Side view of moves 17 & 18, executed with 'Connecting Motion'

Front view of move 36

Side view of move 36

Tips For Yul-Gok Tul

1. For the first movement, some organisations want students to raise their arm/fist straight up, while others require a slow punch.

2. Try to get the timing of the second slow punch inline with stepping out into the sitting stance.

3. For the Elbow Strike, ensure you actually strike your elbow into your palm, as opposed to slapping your elbow with your palm which is incorrect.

4. The jump into X-Stance is a distance jump, with the main foot (right) landing back on your start position and the support foot behind as the 'brake'.

5. The Backfist Strike should be timed and executed as your drop into your final stance, not immediately on landing the first foot of the stance.

Joong-Gun
Korean Patriot

Joong-Gun is named after the patriot Ahn Joong -Gun who assassinated Hiro-Bumi Ito, the first Japanese governor-general of Korea, known as the man who played the leading part in the Korea-Japan merger. The 32 movements in this pattern represent Mr Ahn's age when he was executed at Lui-Shung prison in 1910.

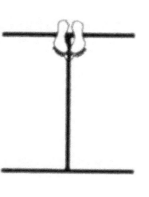

Moa Junbi Sogi 'B'
Closed Ready Stance 'B'

Sonkal Dung Kaunde Makgi
Reverse Knifehand Middle Block

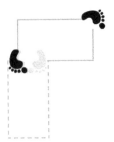

1. From *Moa Junbi Sogi 'B'*, move to your Left into an *L-Stance* and execute a *Reverse Knifehand Middle Block* with your Left hand.

From the Ready Posture to moves 1, 2 & 3

Najunde Ap Cha Busigi
Low Front Snap Kick

Sonbadak Ollyo Makgi
Palm Upward Block

2. Execute a *Low Front Snap Kick* with your front leg (Left), while keeping your arms in the previous block position.

3. Lower your kicking foot in front, then move your Right leg forwards to form a *Left Rear Foot Stance* and execute a *Palm Upward Block* with your Right hand.

Front facing view of the execution of moves 1, 2 & 3

Sonkal Dung Kaunde Makgi
Reverse Knifehand Middle Block

Najunde Ap Cha Busigi
Low Front Snap Kick

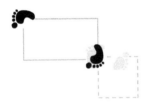

4. Pivot 180 degrees clockwise on your Left foot, moving your Right foot to form a *Left L-Stance* and execute a *Reverse Knifehand Middle Block* with your Right hand.

5. Execute a *Low Front Snap Kick* with your front leg (Right), while keeping your arms in the previous block position.

Moves 4, 5 & 6   Previous

Sonbadak Ollyo Makgi
Palm Upward Block

Kaunde Sonkal Daebi Makgi
Middle Knifehand Guarding Block

Wi Palkup Taeragi
Upper Elbow Strike

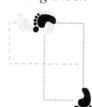

6. Lower your kicking foot in front, then move your Left leg forwards to form a *Right Rear Foot Stance* and execute a *Palm Upward Block* with your Left hand.

7. Pivot 90 degrees anti-clockwise on your right foot to form a *Right L-Stance* and execute a *Middle Knifehand Guarding Block*.

8. Slip into a *Left Walking Stance* (i.e. no stepping) while executing an *Upper Elbow Strike* with your Right elbow. Angle your shoulders so the strike is centred.

Previous

Moves 7 & 8

Kaunde Sonkal Daebi Makgi
Middle Knifehand Guarding Block

Wi Palkup Taeragi
Upper Elbow Strike

Nopunde Sang Sewo Jirugi
High Twin Vertical Punch

9. Move forwards into a *Left L-Stance* and execute a *Middle Knifehand Guarding Block*.

10. Slip into a *Right Walking Stance* (i.e. no stepping) while executing an *Upper Elbow Strike* with your Left elbow. Angle your shoulders so the strike is centred.

11. Move forwards into a *Left Walking Stance* and execute a *High Twin Vertical Punch*

Side view of the execution of the Upward Elbow Strike

Side View of Move 11

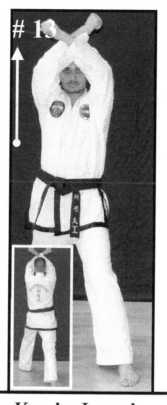

Sang Dwijibo Jirugi
Twin Upset Punch

**Kyocha Joomok
Chookyo Makgi**
X-Fist Rising Block

**Nopunde Dung
Joomok Taeragi**
High Back Fist Strike

12. Move forwards into a *Right Walking Stance* and execute a *Twin Upset Punch*.

13. Using a centre-line turn, pivot 180 degrees anti-clockwise into a *Left Walking Stance* while executing an *X-Fist Rising Block*.

14. Pivot 90 degrees anti-clockwise (to your Left), into a *Right L-Stance* while executing a *High Back Fist Strike* with your Left fist.

Previous *Moves 9, 10, 11, 12, & 13*

Jappyolsol Tae
Release Move

Nopunde Ap Joomok Jirugi
High Section Forefist Punch

ITF Note: Movements 15 & 16 are performed in *'Fast Motion'*

15. Execute a *Release Move* with your Left arm by twisting it anti-clockwise and pulling it downwards and towards your opposite hip. (ITF students bring it straight downwards), whilst simultaneously shifting your front foot to form a Right Walking Stance.

16. Maintain your stance and execute a *High Reverse Forefist Punch* with your Right fist.

Moves 14, 15 & 16 *Previous*

**Nopunde Dung
Joomok Taeragi**
High Back Fist Strike

Jappyolsol Tae
Release Move

ITF Note: Movements 18 & 19 are
performed in *'Fast Motion'*

17. Move your Left foot to your Right (foot to foot) and turn 180 degrees clockwise into a *Left L-Stance* while executing a *High Back Fist Strike* with your Right fist.

18. Execute a *Release Move* with your Right arm by twisting it clockwise and pulling it downwards and towards your opposite hip. (ITF students bring it straight downwards), whilst simultaneously shifting your front foot to form a Left Walking Stance.

Previous   *Moves 17, 18 & 19*

Nopunde Ap Joomok Jirugi
High Section Forefist Punch

Nopunde Doo Palmok Makgi
High Double Forearm Block

Kaunde Ap Joomok Jirugi
Middle Forefist Punch

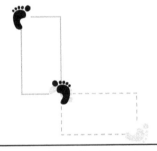

19. Maintain your stance and execute a *High Reverse Forefist Punch* with your Left fist.

20. Move your Right foot to your Left (foot to foot), turn 90 degrees anti-clockwise and step your Left foot forwards to form a *Left Walking Stance* while executing *High Double Forearm Block*.

21. Slip into a *Right L-Stance* (i.e. no stepping) while executing an *Middle Forefist Punch* with your Left fist.

From right to left - Moves 19, 20 & 21 | *Previous*

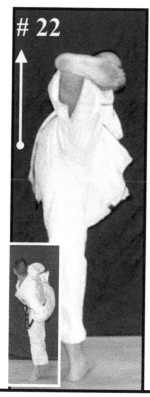

Kaunde Yop Cha Jirugi
Middle Side Piercing Kick

Nopunde Doo Palmok Makgi
High Double Forearm Block

**Kaunde Ap
Joomok Jirugi**
Middle Forefist Punch

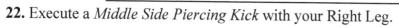

22. Execute a *Middle Side Piercing Kick* with your Right Leg.

23. Lower your foot and land in a *Right Walking Stance* while executing a *High Double Forearm Block*.

24. Slip into a *Left L-Stance* (i.e. no stepping) while executing an *Middle Forefist Punch* with your Right fist.

Previous

Moves 22, 23 & 24

Kaunde Yop Cha Jirugi
Middle Side Piercing Kick

Kaunde Palmok Daebi Makgi
Middle Forearm Guarding Block

Sonbadak Noollo Makgi
Palm Pressing Block
(slow motion)

25. Execute a *Middle Side Piercing Kick* with your Left Leg.

26. Lower your foot and land in a *Right L- Stance* and execute a *Middle Forearm Guarding Block.*

27. Slip your Left foot into a *Left Low Stance* (Nacho Sogi) while executing a *Right Palm Pressing Block.* Performed in slow motion.

Previous

Moves 25, 26 & 27

Kaunde Palmok Daebi Makgi
Middle Forearm Guarding Block

Sonbadak Noollo Makgi
Palm Pressing Block
(slow motion)

Kyockja Jirugi
Angle Punch
(slow motion)

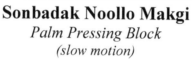

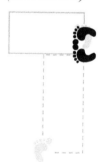

28. Move forwards and form a *Left L-Stance* while executing a *Middle Forearm Guarding Block.*

29. Slip your Right foot into a *Right Low Stance* (Nacho Sogi) while executing a *Left Palm Pressing Block*. Performed in slow motion.

30. Bring your left foot forwards to your right and pivot 90 degrees anti-clockwise into a *Closed Stance* (Moa Sogi) while executing an *Angle Punch* with your Right fist. The fist of the *Angle Punch* aligns with your left shoulder. Perform in slow motion.

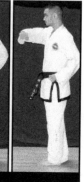

Previous

Moves 28, 29 & 30

Sang Bandalson Digutja Makgi
Twin Arc-hand U Shape Block

Sang Bandalson Digutja Makgi
Twin Arc-hand U Shape Block

31. Move forwards in the direction you are facing, into a *Right Fixed Stance* (Gojang sogi) while executing a *Twin Arc-hand U Shape Block.*

32. Move your Right foot to your Left (foot to foot) and turn 180 anti-degrees clockwise, stepping out with your Left foot to form a *Left Fixed Stance,* while executing a *Twin Arc-hand U Shape Block.*

Executing Angle Punch

Move 31

Previous

Moa Junbi Sogi 'B'
Closed Ready Stance 'B'

Return. Bring Left foot back to *Moa Junbi Sogi 'B'* (the Ready Posture), turning 90 degrees clockwise as you do so.

Previous

Move 32

Back to Ready Posture

Tips For Joong-Gun Tul

1. When performing the *Upper Elbow Strike*, ensure you turn your shoulders so the strike is central and targeted correctly.

2. A common error when transferring from the *X-Fist Rising Block* to the chamber of the *Back Fist Strike* is to pull the arms apart and re-chamber for the Back Fist. Instead, simply lower the arms to a horizontal position to prevent wasted motion.

3. An *Angle Punch* is shoulder height and inline with the opposite shoulder of the hand that is punching.

4. For the *U-Shape Blocks*, ensure your elbow of the lower arm is tucked tight against your body with no space and that the hands are in-line vertically. Be careful not to lean forwards too much.

Frontward view of moves 20, 21, 22 & 23

From Right to Left - Palm Pressing Block from Forearm Guarding Block (Moves 28 & 29)

Toi-Gye
Yi Hwang

Toi-Gye is the pseudonym (penname) of the noted scholar Yi Hwang (16th century A.D.), an authority on neo-Confucianism. Toi-Gye has **37** movements which refer to his birthplace on **37** degrees latitude, and the diagram represents scholar.

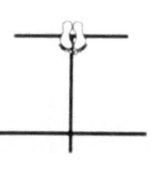

Moa Junbi Sogi 'B'	**Kaunde An Palmok Makgi**	**Dwijibo Sonkut Tulgi**
Closed Ready Stance 'B'	*Middle Inner Forearm Block*	*Upset Fingertip Thrust*

 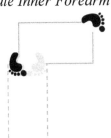 

1. From *Moa Junbi Sogi 'B'*, move to your Left into a *Right L-Stance* and execute a *Middle Inner Forearm Block* with your left arm.

2. Slip your left foot into a *Left Walking Stance*, execute a *Upset Fingertip Thrust*, with your Right hand, pulling Left hand to your Right shoulder.

From the Ready Posture to moves 1, 2 & 3

Dung Joomok
Yop Dwit Taeragi
Backfist Side Back Strike
(slow motion)

Kaunde An Palmok Makgi
Middle Inner Forearm Block

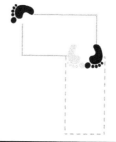

3. Move your Left foot to your Right foot and form a *Closed Stance*. Execute a *Backfist Side Back Strike* with your Right fist, bringing your Left arm into a low block position. Perform in slow motion.

4. Move 90 degrees to your Right into a *Left L-Stance* and execute a *Middle Inner Forearm Block* with your Right arm.

Moves 4, 5 & 6 (from right to left)

Previous

Dwijibo Sonkut Tulgi
Upset Fingertip Thrust

Dung Joomok
Yop Dwit Taeragi
Backfist Side Back Strike
(slow motion)

Kyocha Joomok
Noollo Makgi
X-Fist Pressing Block

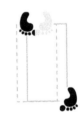

5. Slip your right foot into a *Right Walking Stance*, execute a *Upset Fingertip Thrust* with your Left hand, pulling right hand to your Left shoulder.

6. Move your Right foot to your Left foot and form a *Closed Stance*. Execute a *Backfist Side Back Strike* with your Left fist, bringing your Right arm into a low block position. Perform in slow motion.

7. Move forwards with your Left foot into a *Left Walking Stance* while executing an *X-Fist Pressing Block*.

Nopunde Sang Sewo Jirugi	**Kaunde Ap Cha Busugi**	**Kaunde Ap Joomok Jirugi**
High Twin Vertical Punch	*Middle Front Snap Kick*	*Middle Forefist Punch*

ITF Note: Movements 7 & 8 are performed in *'Continuous Motion'*

8. Maintain your stance and execute a *High Twin Vertical Punch*.

9. Keep your hands in the same position and execute a *Middle Front Snap Kick* with your Right foot.

10. From the kick, land in a *Right Walking Stance* while executing a *Middle Forefist Punch* with your Right fist.

Previous — *Moves 7, 8, 9, 10 & 11*

Kaunde Bandae Ap Joomok Jirugi
Middle Reverse Forefist Punch

Sang Yop Palkup Tulgi
Twin Side Elbow Thrust
(slow motion)

San Makgi
W Block

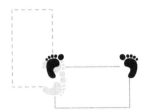

11. Maintain your stance and execute a *Middle Reverse Forefist Punch* with your Left fist.

12. Pivot 90 degrees anti-clockwise on your Right foot, to form a *Closed Stance*, executing a *Twin Side Elbow Thrust*. Perform in slow motion.

13. Pivot 90 degrees anti-clockwise into a *Sitting Stance*, stamping with your Right foot and execute a *W Block*.

Previous

Moves 12 & 13

San Makgi
W Block

San Makgi
W Block

14. Pivot 180 degrees clockwise into a *Sitting Stance*, stamping with your Left foot and execute a *W Block.*

15. Pivot 180 degrees clockwise into a *Sitting Stance*, stamping with your Left foot and execute a *W Block.*

Previous

Moves 14 & 15

San Makgi
W Block

San Makgi
W Block

16. Pivot 180 degrees anti-clockwise into a *Sitting Stance*, stamping with your Right foot and execute a *W Block*.

17. Pivot 180 degrees clockwise into a *Sitting Stance*, stamping with your Left foot and execute a *W Block*.

Moves 16 & 17 (right to left)   *Previous*

San Makgi
W Block

**Doo Palmok Najunde
Mirro Makgi**
*Double Forearm
Low Pushing Block*

Mori Japgi
Head Grab

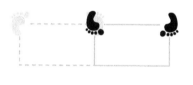 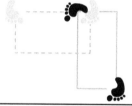 

18. Pivot 180 degrees clockwise into a *Sitting Stance*, stamping with your Left foot and execute a *W Block*.

19. Bring your Right foot in to your Left, then step your Left leg forwards to form a *Right L-Stance* while executing a *Double Forearm Low Pushing Block*.

20. Without moving forwards, slip your Left foot to form a *Left Walking Stance* and execute a *Head Grab* with both hands.

Previous

Moves 18, 19 & 20

Moorup Chagi
Knee Kick

Kaunde Sonkal Daebi Makgi
Middle Knifehand Guarding Block

Najunde Ap Cha Busigi
Low Front Snap Kick

21. Execute a *Right Knee Kick*, pulling hands to your knee as you execute the kick.

22. Bring your Right foot to your Left (foot to foot), then pivot 180 degrees anti-clockwise and move your Left foot forwards to form a *Right L-Stance* while executing a *Middle Knifehand Guarding Block*.

23. Without moving forwards, execute a *Low Front Snap Kick* with your front (Left) foot. Keep your hands in the previous blocking position throughout the kick.

Previous   *Moves 21, 22, 23, 24 & 25*

Opun Sonkut Tulgi
Flat Fingertip Thrust

Kaunde Sonkal Daebi Makgi
Middle Knifehand Guarding Block

Najunde Ap Cha Busigi
Low Front Snap Kick

24. Bring the kicking foot down to form a *Left Walking Stance* and execute a *Flat Fingertip Thrust* with your Left hand.

25. Move forwards into a *Left L-Stance* executing a *Middle Knifehand Guarding Block*.

26. Without moving forwards, execute a *Low Front Snap Kick* with your front (Right) foot. Keep your hands in the previous blocking position throughout the kick.

Side view of moves 21 to 24

Opun Sonkut Tulgi
Flat Fingertip Thrust

**Dung Joomok Taeragi/
Najunde Bakat Palmok Makgi**
*Backfist Strike/
Low Outer Forearm Block*

**Kyocha Joomok
Noollo Makgi**
*X-Fist
Pressing Block*

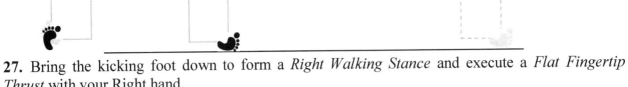

27. Bring the kicking foot down to form a *Right Walking Stance* and execute a *Flat Fingertip Thrust* with your Right hand.

28. Move your Right foot backwards into a *Right L-Stance* , looking back briefly and execute a *Backfist Strike* and *Low section Outer Forearm Block* simultaneously, looking forwards again as you complete the techniques.

29. Jump forwards into a *Right X-Stance* turning 90 degrees anti-clockwise as you do so. Landing while executing a *X-Fist Pressing Block*. Note: This is a height jump.

Previous *Moves 26, 27, 28 & 29*

Nopunde Doo Palmok Makgi
High Double Forearm Block

Najunde Sonkal Daebi Makgi
Low Knifehand Guarding Block

30. Turning 90 degrees clockwise, continue forwards and move your Right leg to form a *Right Walking Stance*, while executing a *High Double Forearm Block.*

31. Pivot 90 degrees anti-clockwise on your Right foot to form a *Right L-Stance* and execute a *Low Knifehand Guarding Block.*

From Right to Left - Moving backwards from move 27 to 28

From Right to Left - Jumping forwards from 28 to 29

An Palmok Dollimyo Makgi
Inner Forearm Circular Block

Najunde Sonkal Daebi Makgi
Low Knifehand Guarding Block

32. Slip your Left foot into a *Left Walking Stance* and execute an *Inner Forearm Circular Block* with your Right arm.

33. Move your Left foot to your Right (foot to foot), turn 180 degrees clockwise and step your Right leg into a *Left L-Stance* and execute a *Low Knifehand Guarding Block*.

Previous — *Moves 30, 31 & 32*

An Palmok Dollimyo Makgi
Inner Forearm Circular Block

An Palmok Dollimyo Makgi
Inner Forearm Circular Block

34. Slip your Right foot into a *Right Walking Stance* and execute an *Inner Forearm Circular Block* with your Left arm.

35. Without stepping, pivot 45 degrees anti-clockwise to form a *45 degree Left Walking Stance* and execute an *Inner Forearm Circular Block* with your Right arm.

Moves 33 & 34 (from right to left)

Previous

An Palmok Dollimyo Makgi
Inner Forearm Circular Block

Kaunde Ap Joomok Jirugi
Middle Forefist Punch

36. Pivot back again to the previous position, again without stepping, forming a *Right Walking Stance* and execute an *Inner Forearm Circular Block* with your Left arm.

37. Move your Right foot anti-clockwise into a Sitting Stance and execute a *Right Middle Forefist Punch*.

Previous   *Moves 35 & 36*

Moa Junbi Sogi 'B'
Closed Ready Stance

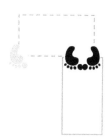

Return. Bring your Right foot back to *Moa Junbi Sogi 'B' (the Ready Posture)*

Previous

Move 37 & back to Ready Posture

Tips For Toi-Gye Tul

1. There is usually little or no hip twist on the first X-Block.

2. Remember the first W Block is the travels anti-clockwise 90 degrees in the direction you are already facing.

3. To remember the correct sequence of W-Blocks, remember 2 - 3 - 1. That's 2 in the direction you start, 3 back in the opposite direction and the last one back again.

4. Following the Knee Kick, bring your foot down next to your other foot as you step and turn to perform the Knifehand Guarding Block.

5. There is no slide when performing the Back Fist Strike, you just take a step back.

6. When performing the jump into X-Stance, be sure to tuck your knees up as it's a height based jump.

7. To ensure you finish on your start position, when performing the jump into X-Stance do so at an diagonal angle (to your left). You will land one shoulder width across and one and a half shoulder widths away from your start position, so with the next stance forwards (a Walking Stance) you will be able to place your right foot back onto your start position.

Saju Tulgi
Four Directional Thrust

사주 막기

Saju Tulgi is the third basic exercise. This is designed to introduce 2nd kup students to sliding into rear elbow thrust techniques as found in the 2nd kup pattern Hwa-Rang. Saju Tulgi has 4 movements repeated in both directions.

Moa Junbi Sogi 'C'
Closed Ready Stance 'C'

Yop Palkup Tulgi
Side Elbow Thrust

Yop Palkup Tulgi
Side Elbow Thrust

1. From the Ready Posture (*Closed Ready Stance 'C'*), pivot 90 degrees anti-clockwise and slide into a *Right L-Stance* whilst executing a *Side Elbow Thrust* with your Right elbow.

2. Pivot 90 degrees anti-clockwise and slide into a *Right L-Stance* whilst executing a *Side Elbow Thrust* with your Right elbow.

From the ready posture to moves 1 & 2

Yop Palkup Tulgi
Side Elbow Thrust

Yop Palkup Tulgi
Side Elbow Thrust

Moa Junbi Sogi 'C'
Closed Ready Stance 'C'

3. Pivot 90 degrees anti-clockwise and slide into a *Right L-Stance* whilst executing a *Side Elbow Thrust* with your Right elbow.

4. Pivot 90 degrees anti-clockwise and slide into a *Right L-Stance* whilst executing a *Side Elbow Thrust* with your Right elbow.

Return. Move your Right foot back to Ready Posture (*Closed Ready Stance 'C'*),

Previous

Moves 3 & 4 and return to Ready Posture

Yop Palkup Tulgi
Side Elbow Thrust

Yop Palkup Tulgi
Side Elbow Thrust

Yop Palkup Tulgi
Side Elbow Thrust

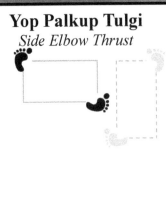

1. From the Ready Posture (*Closed Ready Stance 'C'*), pivot 90 degrees clockwise and slide into a *Left L-Stance* whilst executing a *Side Elbow Thrust* with your Left elbow.

2. Pivot 90 degrees clockwise and slide into a *Left L-Stance* whilst executing a *Side Elbow Thrust* with your Left elbow.

3. Pivot 90 degrees clockwise and slide into a *Left L-Stance* whilst executing a *Side Elbow Thrust* with your Left elbow.

Previous — *Moves 1,2 & 3*

Yop Palkup Tulgi
Side Elbow Thrust

Moa Junbi Sogi 'C'
Closed Ready Stance 'C'

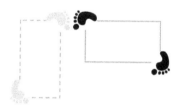
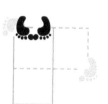

4. Pivot 90 degrees clockwise and slide into a *Left L-Stance* whilst executing a *Side Elbow Thrust* with your Left elbow.

Return. Move your left foot back to Ready Posture (*Closed Ready Stance 'C'*).

Previous   *Move 4 and Return to Ready Posture*

Tips For Saju Tulgi

1. Ensure you have completely turned 90 degrees into the L-Stances.

2. Chamber for the Elbow Thrust during the turn.

3. The 'Elbowing' arm always goes underneath the reaction arm for this exercise.

4. Ensure the 'Elbow' thrust is formed so it runs straight (i.e. Straight back at 180 degrees), rather than angled.

5. Try not to stop between the turn and the actual slide into the 'Elbow Thrust' technique as it should all 'flow'.

Hwa-Rang
Flowering Youth

화
랑
틀

Hwa-Rang is named after the Hwa-Rang youth group, which originated in the Silla Dynasty in the early 7th century. Hwa-Rang has 29 movements which refer to the 29th Infantry Division, where Taekwon-Do developed into maturity.

Moa Junbi Sogi 'C'
Closed Ready Stance 'C'

Kaunde Sonbadak Miro Makgi
Middle Palm Pushing Block

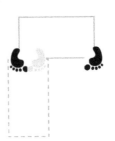

1. From *Moa Junbi Sogi 'C'*, move your Left into a Sitting Stance and execute a *Middle Palm Pushing Block* with your Left hand.

ITF Note: For ITF Students this performed in a straight line directly in front of the left shoulder *(see right)*

Kaunde Ap Joomok Jirugi
Middle Forefist Punch

Kaunde Ap Joomok Jirugi
Middle Forefist Punch

2. Maintain your stance and execute a *Middle Forefist Punch* with your Right fist.

3. Maintain your stance and execute a *Middle Forefist Punch* with your Left fist.

From the Ready Posture to moves 1, 2 & 3

Sang Palmok Makgi
Twin Forearm Block

Ollyo Jirugi
Upward Punch

4. Slip your Right foot out to form a *Left L-Stance* (facing your right) and execute a *Twin Forearm Block*.

5. Relax and extend your Right hand in a grabbing motion and pull it in sharply towards your Left shoulder. As you do this, execute an *Upward Punch* with your Left fist while dropping your weight back into your *L-Stance*. The Punch is performed using a circular motion.

Note: *Some organisations do not perform the grabbing motion and simply withdraw the fist to the shoulder.*

Previous   *Moves 4 & 5*

Gojang Sogi, Kaunde Jirugi
Fixed Stance, Middle Punch

Sonkal Naeryo Taeragi
Knifehand Downward Strike

6. Slide into a *Right Fixed Stance* (approximately 1 stance length to your Right) and execute a *Middle Punch* with your Right fist.

7. Withdraw your Right foot into a *Left Vertical Stance* (Wen Soojik Sogi) and execute a *Knifehand Downward Strike* with your Right hand.

Previous

Moves 6 & 7

Kaunde Ap Joomok Jirugi
Middle Forefist Punch

Najunde Bakat Palmok makgi
Low Outer Forearm Block

Kaunde Ap Joomok Jirugi
Middle Forefist Punch

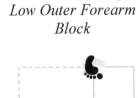
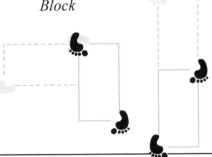

8. Move forwards into a *Left Walking Stance* and execute a *Middle Forefist Punch* with your Left fist.

9. Pivot 90 degrees anti-clockwise into a *Left Walking Stance* and execute a *Low Outer Forearm Block* with your Left arm.

10. Move forwards into a *Right Walking Stance* and execute a *Middle Forefist Punch* with your Right fist.

Previous   *Moves 8, 9, 10 & 11*

**Place Left Palm
Over Right Hand**
Half Step

Kaunde Yop Cha Jirugi / Kaunde Sonkal Yop Taeragi
Middle Side Piercing Kick / Middle Knifehand Side Strike

11. Move your Left foot half way towards your Right, whilst simultaneously placing your Left palm over your Right fist, bending your Right elbow about 45 degrees.

12a. From the previous position, execute a *Middle Side Piercing Kick* while pulling your hands in the opposite direction.

12b. Following the kick, land in a *Left L-Stance* and execute a *Middle Knifehand Side Strike* with your Right hand.

Note: 12A and 12B were counted as a single move by General Choi.

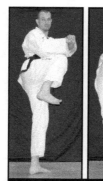

Previous

Moves 12a, 12b, 13 & 14

Kaunde Ap Joomok Jirugi
Middle Forefist Punch

Kaunde Ap Joomok Jirugi
Middle Forefist Punch

Kaunde Sonkal Daebi Makgi
Middle Knifehand Guarding Block

13. Move forwards into a *Left Walking Stance* and execute a *Middle Forefist Punch* with your Left fist.

14. Move forwards into a *Right Walking Stance* and execute a *Middle Forefist Punch* with your Right fist.

15. Pivot 90 degrees anti-clockwise into a *Right L-Stance* and execute a *Middle Knifehand Guarding Block*.

Previous
Moves 15, 16 & 17

Sun Sonkut Tulgi
Straight Fingertip Thrust

Kaunde Sonkal Daebi Makgi
Middle Knifehand Guarding Block

16. Move forwards into a *Right Walking Stance* while executing a *Straight Fingertip Thrust* with your Right hand.

17. Perform a centre-line turn to face the opposite direction in a *Right L-Stance* and execute a *Middle Knifehand Guarding Block*.

Previous

Moves 18, 19a & 19b

Nopunde Dollyo Chagi
High Turning Kick

Nopunde Dollyo Chagi
High Turning Kick

ITF Note: Movements 18 & 19 are performed in *'Fast Motion'* and at 30 degree angles

18. Execute a *High Turning Kick* with your Right leg.

19a. Execute a *High Turning Kick* with your Left leg.

Note: There is no official distance for the placement of your right foot following the fist kick, but the kicking foot should end up approximately one shoulder width away from the standing foot.

Note: Some organisations like you to hold the Knifehand Guarding Block (Move 17) while kicking, whilst others prefer a closed fist guard position.

Previous

Moves 20, 21, 22 & 23

Kaunde Sonkal Daebi Makgi
Middle Knifehand Guarding Block

Najunde Bakat Palmok Makgi
Low Outer Forearm Block

Kaunde Jirugi
Middle Punch

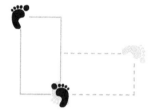

19b. Bring the kicking foot down to form a *Right L-Stance* and execute a *Middle Knifehand Guarding Block* with your Left hand.
Note: 19A and 19B were counted as a single move by General Choi.

20. Pivot 90 degrees anti-clockwise on your Right foot into a *Left Walking Stance* and execute a *Low Outer Forearm Block* with your Left arm.

21. Without moving forwards, slip your Left foot to form a *Right L-Stance* and execute a *Middle Punch* with your Right fist.

Frontward View Of Moves 20 to 23

Kaunde Jirugi
Middle Punch

Kaunde Jirugi
Middle Punch

**Kyocha Joomok
Noollo Makgi**
*X-Fist
Pressing Block*

22. Move forwards into a *Left L-Stance* and execute a *Middle Punch* with your Left fist.

23. Move forwards into a *Right L-Stance* and execute a *Middle Punch* with your Right fist.

24. Without moving forwards, slip your Left foot to form a *Left Walking Stance* and execute an *X-Fist Pressing Block*.

Previous   *Moves 24 & 25*

Yop Palkup Tulgi
Side Elbow Thrust

**An Palmok Yop Ap Makgi /
Najunde Bakat Palmok Makgi**
*Inner Forearm Side Front Block /
Low Out Forearm Block*

25. Pivoting 180 degrees anti-clockwise, slide towards start position to form a *Right L-Stance* and execute a *Side Elbow Thrust* with your Right elbow.

26. Pivot 90 degrees anti-clockwise, bringing your Left foot in to your Right to form *a Closed Stance*, chambering for the next technique as you do so. Upon completion of the turn, execute a *High Inner Forearm Side Front Block* with your Right arm and a *Low Outer Forearm Block* with your Left arm - simultaneously.

Frontward View Of Moves 24, 25 & 26

**An Palmok Yop Ap Makgi /
Najunde Bakat Palmok Makgi**
*Inner Forearm Side Front Block /
Low Out Forearm Block*

Kaunde Sonkal Daebi Makgi
Middle Knifehand Guarding Block

---

27. Maintain your stance (but rise and drop on toes) and execute a *High Inner Forearm Side Front Block* with your Left arm and a *Low Outer Forearm Block* with your Right arm - simultaneously.

28. Move forwards with your Left foot to form a *Right L-Stance* and execute a *Middle Knifehand Guarding Block*.

Previous   *Moves 27 & 28*

Kaunde Sonkal Daebi Makgi
Middle Knifehand Guarding Block

Moa Junbi Sogi 'C'
Closed Ready Stance 'C'

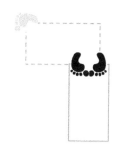

---

29. Move foot to foot (Left to Right foot) turning 180 degrees clockwise to form a *Left L-Stance* and execute a *Middle Knifehand Guarding Block*.

Return. Bring your Right foot back to the Ready Posture (*Closed Ready Stance 'C'*)

Side Front Blocks With Chambering

Previous

Move 28 & Return

Tips For Hwa-Rang Tul

1. When travelling back to your start position be careful not to over exaggerate your L-Stances when performing the middle punches.

2. Ensure you complete the last L-Stance with punch before slipping into the X-Block.

3. When performing the Rear Elbow Strike, it is common to see the elbow angled rather than pointing straight back. Students do not realise that it is at an angle as it feels comfortable to them and they cannot see it properly. To be correct it should be pointing straight back, which usually means moving your arm (not your fist) a little further away from the body.

4. When performing the Side Front Block combinations, be careful not to make the first chamber (with your left arm) look like a block by keeping it relaxed as you turn and not locking it into position.

5. For the Side Front Block combinations, the arm that travels downwards always goes inside the other arm.

Choong-Moo

Admiral Yi Sun-sin

Choong-Moo has 30 movements. Choong-Moo was the name given to the great Admiral Yi Sun-sin of the Lee Dynasty. He was reputed to have invented the first armoured battleship (Kobukson) in 1592, which is said to be the precursor of the present day submarine.

The reason why this pattern ends with a left hand attack is to symbolize his regrettable death, having no chance to show his unrestrained potentiality, checked by the forced reservation of his loyalty to the king.

Narani Junbi Sogi
Parallel Ready Stance

Sang Sonkal Makgi
Twin Knifehand Block

Sonkal Nopunde Ap Taeragi
Knifehand High Front Strike

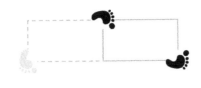

1. From *Narani Junbi Sogi*, move your Left foot to form *Right L-Stance* and execute a *Twin Knifehand Block*.

2. Move forwards into a *Right Walking Stance* and execute a *Knifehand High Front Strike* with your Right hand while bringing your Left hand (flat) in front of your forehead, palm facing forward.

From the Ready Posture to moves 1 & 2

196

Kaunde Sonkal Daebi Makgi
Middle Knifehand Guarding Block

Nopunde Opun Sonkut Tulgi
High Flat Fingertip Thrust

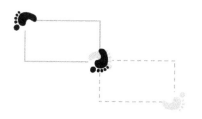

3. Turn 180 degrees, pivoting clockwise on your Left foot into a *Left L-Stance* and execute a *Middle Knifehand Guarding Block.*

4. Move forwards into a *Left Walking Stance* and execute a *High Flat Fingertip Thrust.*

Moves 3 & 4 (right to left)

Previous

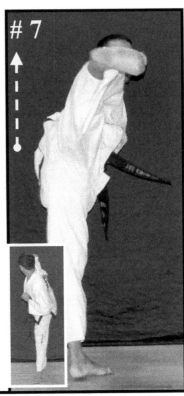

Kaunde Sonkal Daebi Makgi
Middle Knifehand Guarding Block

Goburyo Junbi Sogi 'A'
Bending Ready Stance 'A'

Kaunde Yop Cha Jirugi
Middle Side Piercing Kick

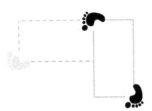

5. Pivot 90 degrees anti-clockwise on your Right foot (moving your left foot) to form a *Right L-Stance* and execute a *Middle Knifehand Guarding Block*.

6. Taking your weight on your Left leg, turn 180 degrees clockwise (to face the start position) and form a *Left Bending Ready Stance 'A'*.

7. From the Bending Ready Stance execute a *Middle Side Piercing Kick* with your Right leg.

Previous

Moves 5, 6, 7 & 8

**Kaunde Sonkal
Daebi Makgi**
*Middle Knifehand
Guarding Block*

Twimyo Yop Cha Jirugi
Flying Side Piercing Kick

**Kaunde Sonkal
Daebi Makgi**
*Middle Knifehand
Guarding Block*

8. Following the Side Piercing Kick, place your Right foot down to form a Right L-Stance, facing 180 degrees in the opposite direction from where you just kicked and execute a *Middle Knifehand Guarding Block*.

9a. Take a step forwards with your Right foot and execute a *Flying Side Piercing Kick* with your Right leg. This is performed in *'double motion'* (or *'bicycle motion'*), by raising your Left knee into the air' This helps pull your weight up in to the air in order to gain height. At the peak of the jump execute the *Flying Side Piercing Kick* with your Right leg.

9b. Land in a *Left L-Stance* and execute a *Middle Knifehand Guarding Block*.
Note*: 9A and 9B were counted as a single move by General Choi.*

Previous

Moves 7 & 8

Najunde Bakat Palmok Makgi
Low Outer Forearm Block

Mori Japgi
Head Grab

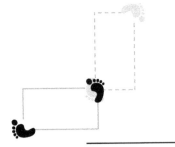

10. Pivot foot 270 degrees anti-clockwise on your Right foot, to form a *Right L-Stance* and execute a *Low Outer Forearm Block* with your Left arm.

11. Without moving forwards, slip your Left foot to form a *Left Walking Stance* while executing a *Head Grab* with both hands.

Moorup Chagi
Knee Kick

Nopunde Sonkal Dung Ap Taeragi
High Reverse Knifehand Front Strike

12. Execute a *Right Knee Kick*, pulling your hands onto your knee as its executed.

13. Following the Knee Kick, bring your Right foot down to your Left foot. Turn 180 degrees anti-clockwise and move forwards with your Left foot to form a *Left Walking Stance.* Execute a *High Reverse Knifehand Front Strike* with your Right hand, bringing your Left hand (flat with palm down) underneath your Right elbow.

Previous   *Moves 10, 11, 12 & 13*

Nopunde Dollyo Chagi
High Turning Kick

Kaunde Dwitcha Jirugi
Middle Back Piercing Kick

ITF Note: Movements 14 & 15 are performed in *'Fast Motion'* and Movement 14 is performed at a 30 degree angle

14. Perform a *High Turning Kick* with your Right leg

15. Land foot to foot and perform a *Middle Back Piercing Kick* with your Left leg.

Previous   *Moves 14, 15 & 16*

**Kaunde Palmok
Daebi Makgi**
Middle Forearm Guarding Block

Kaunde Dollyo Chagi
Middle 45° Turning Kick

**Sang Bandalson
Digutja Makgi**
*Twin Arc-hand
U-Shape Block*

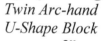
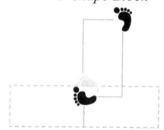

16. Lower your Left leg as you turn 180 degrees to form a *Left L-Stance* and execute a *Middle Forearm Guarding Block.*

17. Execute a *Left Middle Turning Kick* at a 45 degree angle.

18. Lower your kicking leg foot to foot and step your Right leg forward (towards your start position) to form a *Right Fixed Stance* and execute a *Twin Arc-Hand U-Shape Block.*

Previous

Moves 17 & 18

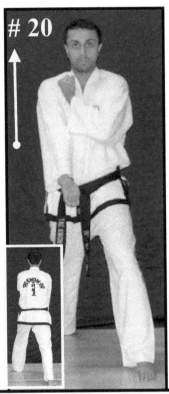

Kaunde Sonkal Daebi Makgi
Middle Knifehand Guarding Block

Dwijibo Sonkut Tulgi
Upset Fingertip Thrust

Dung Joomok Taeragi / Najunde Bakat Palmok Makgi
Back Fist Strike / Low Outer Forearm Block

19. Jump *(Twigi)* on the spot and spin 360 degrees anti-clockwise, landing in a *Left L-Stance* while executing a *Middle Knifehand Guarding Block.* The block should be performed <u>as</u> you land.

20. Move forwards into a *Left Walking Stance*, while executing an *Upset Fingertip Thrust* with your Right hand, bringing your left fist to your Right shoulder.

21. Shift your Right leg to form a *Right L-Stance* while simultaneously executing a *Back Fist Strike* with your Right fist and a *Low Outer Forearm Block* with your Left arm.

Previous   *Move 19 & 20*

Sun Sonkut Tulgi
Straight Fingertip Thrust

Nopunde Doo Palmok Makgi
High Double Forearm Block

22. Move forwards into a *Right Walking Stance* and execute a *Straight Fingertip Thrust* with your Right hand.

23. Pivot 270 degrees anti-clockwise on your Right foot to form a *Left Walking Stance* and execute a *High Double Forearm Block*.

Previous

Moves 21, 22 & 23

Palmok Kaunde Ap Makgi
Forearm Middle Front Block

Nopunde Dung Joomok Yop Taeragi
High Back Fist Side Strike

24a. Move your Right foot forwards to form a *Sitting Stance* and execute a *Forearm Middle Front Block* with your Right arm.

24b. Immediately execute a *High Back Fist Side Strike* with your Right arm, maintaining the same stance from the previous move.

Note: 24A and 24B were counted as a single move by General Choi.

Kaunde Yop Cha Jirugi
Middle Side Piercing Kick

25. Execute a *Middle Side Piercing Kick* with your Right Leg, in the opposite direction (180 degrees) from your previous Back fist.

Previous   *Moves 24 (A & B) & 25*

Kaunde Yop Cha Jirugi
Middle Side Piercing Kick

Kyocha Sonkal
Kaunde Makgi
X-Knifehand Middle Block

> **ITF Note:** Movement 27 is now performed as an X-Knifehand Checking Block *(Kyocha Sonkal Momchau Makgi)* and comes straight out from chest

---

26. Lower your Right foot approximately 1 shoulder width from your Left foot and execute a *Middle Side Piercing Kick* with your Left leg.

27. Lower your Left foot approximately 1 shoulder width from your Right foot and turn 180 degrees clockwise. Slide your Right leg forwards into a *Left L-Stance*, executing a *X-Knifehand Middle Block*.

> **ITF Note:** For ITF students movement this is a *X-Knifehand Checking Block* (Kyocha Sonkal Momchau Makgi) and comes straight out from chest height.

Previous

Moves 26 & 27

Doo Sonbadak Ollyo Makgi
Double Palm Upward Block

Chookyo Makgi
Rising Block

28. Move forwards into a *Left Walking Stance* and execute a *Double Palm Upward Block*.

29. Perform a centre line turn to form a *Right Walking Stance* and execute a *Rising Block* with your Right arm.

Previous

Moves 28, 29, 30 & return to Ready Stance

30

Kaunde Bandae Ap Joomok Jirugi
Middle Reverse Forefist Punch

Narani Junbi Sogi
Parallel Ready Stance

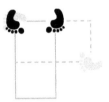

30. Maintain your stance and execute a *Middle Reverse Forefist Punch* with your Left arm.

Return. Bring your Left foot back to the Ready Posture (*Narani Junbi Sogi*)

Tips For Choong-Moo Tul

1. On move #2, the Left hand (the one that is placed in front of your forehead, almost flicks into position.

2. The Flying Side Piercing Kick in double motion (bicycle motion) is a fairly hard technique to perform. Isolate it from the pattern and practice it separately for the best performance.

3. The key to successfully completing the 360 degree jump is to tuck your knees up high as you jump/spin. All too often I see students try to do it with almost straight leg which makes it very hard to complete fully. Also, throws your hands back (in the chamber position for Knifehand Guarding block) and keep them there throughout the spin, bringing them forwards simultaneously as you land.

4. Move #21 (the step back and execute a Back Fist strike) doesn't have a slide, it is simply a step.

5. Following the second Side Piercing Kick (move #26), bring the kicking foot about a shoulder width away from your Right foot as this allows you to turn and slide the Right foot into the next L-Stance while executing the X-Knifehand Blocks.

Kwang-Gae

19th King of the Koguryo Dynasty

Kwang-Gae is named after the famous Kwang-Gae-Toh-Wang, the 19th King of the Koguryo Dynasty who regained all the lost territories including the greater part of Manchuria. The diagram represents the expansion and recovery of lost territory. Kwang-Gae has 39 movements which refer to the first two figures of 391 A. D., the year he came to the throne.

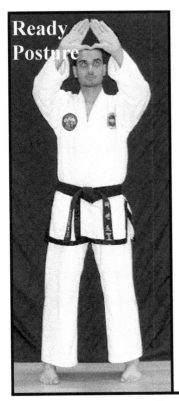

Narani Sogi Hanulson
*Parallel Stance
with Heaven Hand*

Pull both hands out sharply
Raise left foot

Moa Junbi Sogi 'B'
Closed Ready Stance 'B'

1a. From *Parallel Stance with Heaven Hand*, pull both hands sharply outwards (using Knifehands), taking your weight on your Right foot and extending your Left foot outwards.

1b. Bring your hands around in a circular motion, whilst simultaneously bringing your Left foot back in to form a *Closed Ready Stance 'B'*.

Note: *1a and 1b were counted as a single move by General Choi.*

From the ready posture to move 1 (A & B)

Dwijibo Jirugi
Upset Punch
(slow motion)

Dwijibo Jirugi
Upset Punch
(slow motion)

**Nopunde Sonbadak
Golcha Makgi**
High Palm Hooking Block

2. Move your Left foot forwards to form a *Left Walking Stance* while executing an *Upset Punch* with your Right arm. This is performed in slow motion.

3. Move your Right foot forwards to form a *Right Walking Stance* while executing an *Upset Punch* with your Left arm. This is performed in slow motion.

4. Perform a double stepping motion by stepping your Left foot past your Right, turning your foot outwards, then step your Right foot forwards into a *Right Walking Stance* while executing a *Palm Hooking Block* with your Right hand. This motion is known as *'Double Stepping Forwards'* (Ibo Omgyo Didimyo Nagagi)

Previous

Moves 2, 3 & 4

**Sonkal Najunde
Daebi Makgi**
*Low Knifehand
Guarding Block*

**Nopunde Sonbadak
Golcha Makgi**
High Palm Hooking Block

**Sonkal Najunde
Daebi Makgi**
*Low Knifehand
Guarding Block*

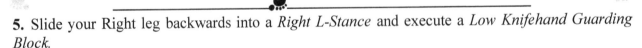

5. Slide your Right leg backwards into a *Right L-Stance* and execute a *Low Knifehand Guarding Block*.

6. Perform a double stepping motion by stepping your Right foot past your Left, turning your foot outwards, then step your Left foot forwards into a *Left Walking Stance* while executing a *Palm Hooking Block* with your Left hand. This motion is known as *'Double Stepping Forwards'* (Ibo Omgyo Didimyo Nagagi)

7. Slide your Left leg backwards into a *Left L-Stance* and execute a *Low Knifehand Guarding Block*.

Previous   *Moves 6, 7 & 8*

**Nopunde Sonkal
Daebi Makgi**
*High Knifehand
Guarding Block*

**Nopunde Sonkal
Daebi Makgi**
*High Knifehand
Guarding Block*

**Sonbadak
Ollyo Makgi**
*Palm Upward Block
(slow motion)*

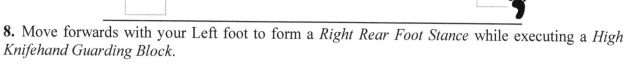

8. Move forwards with your Left foot to form a *Right Rear Foot Stance* while executing a *High Knifehand Guarding Block*.

9. Move forwards with your Right foot to form a *Left Rear Foot Stance* while executing a *High Knifehand Guarding Block*.

10. Perform a double step/turn motion by moving your Left foot past your Right, then pivoting 180 degrees on your Left foot into a *Left Walking Stance*, sliding your Right foot back after the turn to form the stance, while executing a *Palm Upward Block* with your right hand. This motion is known as *'Forward Double Step Turning'* (Apuro Ibo Omgyo Didimyo Dolgi). This is performed in slow motion.

Previous | *Moves 9, 10 & 11*

Sonbadak Ollyo Makgi
Palm Upward Block
(slow motion)

Sonkal Najunde Ap Makgi
Knifehand Low Front Block

11. Move forwards in to a *Right Walking Stance* and execute a *Palm Upward Block* with your Left hand. This is performed in slow motion.

12. Bring your Left foot to your Right to form a *Closed Stance*, while executing a *Knifehand Low Front Block* with your Right Knifehand, hitting the palm of your left hand. This is performed in a circular motion with both hands.

Previous   *Moves 11 & 12*

Outward Pressing Kick
Bakuro Noollo Chagi

Kaunde Yop Cha Jirugi
Middle Side Piercing Kick

13. Keep your hands in the previous position and execute an *Outward Pressing Kick* with your Left leg.

14. Without placing your kicking foot down, immediately execute a *Middle Side Piercing Kick* with your Left leg, keeping your hands in the same position. This motion (13 & 14) is known as a *'Consecutive Kick'* (Yonsok Chagi)

Previous   *Moves 13, 14 & 15*

**Nopunde Sonkal
Anuro Taeragi**
High Knifehand Inward Strike

Yop Joomok Naerjo Taeragi
Side Fist Downward Strike

15. Lower the kick to form a *Right L-Stance* (in the direction of the kick) and execute a *High Knifehand Inward Strike* with your with your Right hand, pulling your Left first into your Right shoulder.

16. Withdraw your Left foot to your Right to form a *Closed Stance*, while executing a *Side Fist Downward Strike* with your Left fist.

Previous   *Moves 16, 17 & 18*

Outward Pressing Kick
Bakuro Noollo Chagi

Kaunde Yop Cha Jirugi
Middle Side Piercing Kick

17. Keep your hands in the previous position and execute an *Outward Pressing Kick* with your Right leg.

18. Without placing your kicking foot down, immediately execute a *Middle Side Piercing Kick* with your Right leg keeping your hands in the same position. This motion (17 & 18) is known as a *'Consecutive Kick'* (Yonsok Chagi)

Previous

Moves 19 & 20

**Sonkal Nopunde
Anuro Taeragi**
Knifehand High Inward Strike

Yop Joomok Naerjo Taeragi
Side Fist Downward Strike

19. Lower the kick to form a *Left L-Stance* (in the direction of the kick) and execute a *High Knifehand Inward Strike* with your with your Left hand, pulling your Right first into your Left shoulder.

20. Withdraw your Right foot to your Left to form a *Closed Stance*, while executing a *Side Fist Downward Strike* with your Right fist.

Previous

Moves 21, 22 & 23

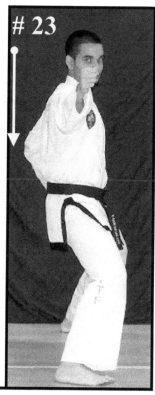

Sonbadak Noollo Makgi
Palm Pressing Block
(slow motion)

Sonbadak Noollo Makgi
Palm Pressing Block
(slow motion)

Nopunde Dung Joomok Yop Taeragi
High Back Fist Side Strike

21. Move your Left foot forwards into a *Left Low Stance* while executing a *Palm Pressing Block* with your Right hand. Perform in slow motion.

22. Move your Right foot forwards into a *Right Low Stance* while executing a *Palm Pressing Block* with your Left hand. Perform in slow motion.

23. Lift your Right foot and rotate 180 degrees clockwise, *stamping* down into a *Sitting Stance* and execute a *High Back Fist Side Strike* with your Right fist.

Previous

Moves 24, 25 & 26

Kaunde Doo Palmok Magki
Middle Double Forearm Block

Palmok Najunde Bandae Makgi
Forearm Low Reverse Block

Opun Sonkut Tulgi
Flat Fingertip Thrust
(slow motion)

24. Without moving forwards, step your Right (Front) foot outwards to form a *Right Walking Stance* and execute a *Middle Double Forearm Block*.

25. Shifting backwards in the same stance (*Right Walking Stance*), execute a *Forearm Low Reverse Block* with your Left arm while keeping your Right arm in the previous position. Shift backwards about 1 shoulder width. This motion is known as a *'Foot Shifting Backwards'* (Durogamyo Jajunbal).

26. Slip your Right foot forwards into a *Right Low Stance* and execute a *Flat Fingertip Thrust* with your Right hand. Perform in slow motion.

Moves 24 to 25 - Showing the hand positions & slide backwards

**Nopunde Dung
Joomok
Yop Taeragi**
*High Back Fist
Side Strike*

**Kaunde Doo
Palmok Magki**
Middle Double Forearm Block

**Palmok Najunde
Bandae Makgi**
*Forearm Low
Reverse Block*

27. Lift your Left (back) foot and rotate it anti-clockwise so its inline with your right foot. *Stamp* it down into a *Sitting Stance* and execute a *High Back Fist Side Strike* with your Left fist.

28. Without moving forwards, pivot on your Left foot whilst moving your Right (Rear) foot outwards to form a *Left Walking Stance* and execute a *Middle Double Forearm Block*.

29. Shifting backwards in the same stance (*Left Walking Stance*), execute a *Forearm Low Reverse Block* with your Right arm while keeping your Left arm in the previous position. Shift backwards about 1 shoulder width. This motion is known as a *'Foot Shifting Backwards'* (Durogamyo Jajunbal)

Previous   *Moves 27, 28, 29 & 30*

Opun Sonkut Tulgi
Flat Fingertip Thrust

Nopunde Sang Sewo Jirugi
High Twin Vertical Punch

Sang Dwijibo Jirugi
Twin Upset Punch

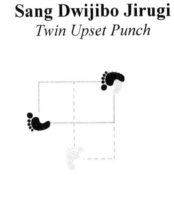

30. Slip your Left foot forwards into a *Left Low Stance* and execute a *Flat Fingertip Thrust* with your Left hand. Perform in slow motion.

31. Moving forwards, *stamp* your Right foot into a *Right Walking Stance* while executing a *High Twin Vertical Punch*.

32. Pivot 90 degrees anti-clockwise on your Right foot and *stamp* into a *Left Walking Stance* while executing a *Twin Upset Punch*.

Previous | *Moves 31 & 32*

Kaunde Ap Cha Busigi
Middle Front Snap Kick

**Kaunde Sonkal
Daebi Makgi**
Middle Knifehand Guarding Block

33. Execute a *Middle Front Snap Kick* with your Right leg keeping your hands in the previous position.

34. Land foot to foot (bring your kicking leg in to your support leg), pivot 180 degrees clockwise and step your Left foot backwards to form a *Left L-Stance*, executing a *Middle Knifehand Guarding Block*.

Previous

Moves 33 & 34

Nopunde Ap Joomok Jirugi
High Forefist Punch

Sang Dwijibo Jirugi
Twin Upset Punch

---

35. Move forwards into a *Left Walking Stance* and execute a *High Punch* with your Left hand.

36. Move forwards, *stamping* into a *Right Walking Stance* while executing a *Twin Upset Punch*.

Previous — *Moves 35 & 36*

Kaunde Ap Cha Busigi
Middle Front Snap Kick

Kaunde Sonkal Daebi Makgi
Middle Knifehand Guarding Block

37. Execute a *Middle Front Snap Kick* with your Left leg keeping your hands in the previous position.

38. Land foot to foot (bring your kicking leg to your support foot), pivot 180 degrees anti-clockwise and step your Right foot backwards to form a *Right L-Stance*, executing a *Middle Knifehand Guarding Block*.

Previous

Moves 37 & 38

Nopunde Ap Joomok Jirugi
High Forefist Punch

Narani Sogi Hanulson
*Parallel Stance
with Heaven Hand*

39. Move forwards into a *Right Walking Stance* and execute a *High Punch* with your Right hand.

Return. Bring your Left foot back to the Ready Posture.

Previous

Moves 39 & return to Ready Stance

Tips For Kwang-Gae Tul

1. On move #1, focus should be on the two knifehands, coming out sharply then moved in a circular motion, as the left leg is simply raised outwards and is not actually a kick.

2. When performing moves #4 and #6 be sure to keep your stance widths during the steps. It is common to step at a slight angle due to moving the stepping foot too close to the other.

3. On move #10 it is the rear foot that slides backwards to form the stance, while on move #11 it is the front foot that slides forwards to form the stance.

4. On moves #13 and #14 the hands stay in the previous position (of move #13) while both kicks are executed, only moving for the chamber of move #15.

5. On moves #17 and #18 the hands stay in the previous position (of move #16) while both kicks are executed, only moving for the chamber of move #19.

6. On moves #25 and #29 try to keep the right and left arms (the one forming the higher part of the previous Double Forearm Blocks) as stationary as possible. What this means is that following the previous move, only the arm performing the Low Block moves. It is common to move the 'high' arm down and then lock it back to its previous position when in fact it is not meant to move at all.

7. Remember, moves #23, #27, #31, #32 and #36 all involve stamping into your stance.

8. Remember, moves #5, 7#, #25 and #25 all involve sliding (about 6 inches) backwards into your stance.

9. Following the front snap kicks (moves #33 and #37) many students get confused about which way to turn, but if you remember that your turn to the side of the leg that just kicked (after stepping foot to foot) you will rotate in the correct direction before sliding the rear leg back into an L-Stance.

Appendices

'Glory is temporary.
Wisdom lasts forever.
Train for a deeper understanding of yourself'

Pattern Speeds

By Master Paul McPhail, 7th Degree, ITFNZ

The follow is a study of the various speeds in patterns, such as fast and continuous motion, and how the ITF perform sine wave. "In the beginning", there was only *normal*, *fast* and *slow* motion. *Continuous* came later, then finally *connecting* with the publishing of the second edition of the 15 volume Encyclopedia in 1983.

There is generally no problem with understanding slow and connecting motion... *connecting* being two movements in the one sinewave and one breath...like hooking block/punch in Yul-Gok, scooping block/punch in Ge-Baek.

But what is the difference between fast and continuous motion?
Is it the sine wave? Is it the breathing? Is it the overall speed or time it takes to complete the movements? Is it the interval of time between the two movements? Let's look at these one by one:

Sine Wave

With the *continuous motion* in Dun-Gun, General Choi gave very clear instructions to drop down after the low block, then rise up, then down on the rising block. In other words, *full sine wave*. Down-up-down. In Po-Eun however, every *continuous* movement is NOT done with full sinewave - the final "down" of the preceding movement becomes the first "down" of the next. So there is no clear rule there. There is also the fast motion in Ul-Ji which is just one movement - dropping into x-stance...so how can we make a clear rule to do with sinewave? Then there is fast motion with kicks also - like in Hwa-Rang and Choong-Moo...

The ITF Technical Committee also offered this definition of *continuous motion* and *sine wave* at the seminar in New Zealand, August 2004: Movements in *continuous motion* should be completed using *full sine wave* (down-up-down) unless there are more than 2 movements (eg Po-Eun 6-12, 24-30 and Yoo-Sin 16-19), in which case perform a *2/3 sine wave*. This definition holds true on my chart in the Sine wave study displayed later.

Breathing

Both *fast* and *continuous* movements call for individual breaths...although the General tended to "merge" his breaths somewhat on continuous motion. The ITF

Technical Committee further explained *continuous motion* breathing as inhaling only once, then breathing out on each technique as you execute it. (NZ seminar, August 2004). *Connecting motion* has only one breath.

It should be noted (just to confuse things) that there appears to be a mistake in the Encyclopedia. It says in the *Theory of Power* section that each movement should have one breath except for *"continuous motion"*. This I think is an error, as it states in the Training Secret section *"except on connecting motion"*.

Over-all Speed or Time Taken

Sometimes *continuous* movements take longer to complete than *fast* - sometimes the other way around. For example, the two *fast motion* punches in Do-San are over and done with quicker than the low/rising blocks in Dan-Gun. Yet in Po-Eun, the *continuous motion* techniques are completed at a fast rate.

Interval Between Movements

There is a popular view that the difference between *normal, fast* and *continuous* is the interval, or gap BETWEEN the movements. The idea is that two movements performed at *normal speed* would have a natural count or gap between them, *fast* has this gap shortened, the *continuous* has no gap at all. This would fine except that this is not the way *fast motion* gets performed, either by seniors, Masters or General Choi himself. If you watch, there is no gap at all between the two punches in Do-san for example... as soon as the first is finished you spring straight up into the 2nd... almost in a *continuous-like* motion.

In my discussions with General Choi, I came across what I think it is all about. I asked him - *"why not just get rid of Continuous and just call everything Fast? Don't you mean just go fast - join them together - cut out the interval between movements?"*

"No no - fast motion is performed with urgency, - aggressive. Continuous motion is performed with grace and beauty - it must flow." he replied.

So I think then, we have to try and understand what his thoughts were when he introduced the terminology. He had *"fast motion"* already - but it didn't adequately describe the flowing, continuous nature by which he wanted certain other movements linked. I don't believe he gave that much thought to there being any confusion over the two terms, as in his mind they are totally different.

If you look then...continuous movements always involve defence - and the idea is to link them smoothly with a nice flow and rhythm. Fast techniques are normally attacks, nearly always punches and kicks (but not always - Yoo Sin 34-35).

Okay, that's all very well, until you have to teach your 1st dans Ge-Baek, where we have *fast* then *continuous* motion side by side. I tend to give a few guidelines, which make people feel more comfortable with the differences. This then is the general summary I use:

Conclusion

Slow Motion - movement is performed slowly with slow breathing. This is used to emphasize an important movement and to check balance and control.

Fast Motion - urgent and aggressive, normal breathing. Fast motion is nearly always attacks - mainly two punches. Short-cut your sine wave - spring straight from the first movement into the next.

Continuous Motion - link the movements together with no pause between the end of one movement and the start of the next. Breath in once then out in a continuous flow of air but emphasizing each movement. Try to link the moments smoothly, with grace and beauty. (Continuous movements always start with a block).

Connecting Motion - complete the two movements with one breath and one sine wave. Connecting motion is always with two movements using opposite arms.

There is also other terminology used in patterns like - ***"in a quick motion, a releasing motion, in a consecutive kick"*** etc. How is a *quick motion* different from a *fast motion*? I asked the General is it the same... he laughed and said *"no no"* ...but gave no explanation!

My thoughts with these are:

- ***"Releasing Motion",*** the General is telling us it is a releasing technique.

- ***"Consecutive Kick",*** the General is telling us *"do not put your foot on the ground after the first kick"*.

- ***"Quick"*** - used for single movements so means *"do it quickly"*, as opposed *to fast motion*, which describes how two or more movements should be performed together.

Pattern Orders of Taekwon-Do Organisations

All organisations that have a link back to General Choi and the Ch'ang Hon patterns utilize them as part of their training and gradings. However, certain organisations have them in different orders due to the time they either left the ITF or for other reasons for example the way their Chief Instructor may have learned them. These lists represent the pattern orders of various big Taekwon-do organisations, with further breakaway groups usually following the exact same sequence.

The following organisational lists appear on the next few pages:

International Taekwon-Do Federation (ITF)
For ITF and Ch'ang Hon organisations that follow the ITF order of patterns.

Global Taekwon-Do Federation (GTF)
For GTF and other organisations that follow the patterns as directed by the late Grandmaster Park, Jung Tae.

Action International Martial Arts Association (AIMAA)
For AIMAA students and other organisations those that follow the patterns as directed by the Grandmaster Hee, Il Cho.

Grandmaster Jhoon Rhee
For students of Grandmaster Jhoon Rhee and organisations that follow the same order of patterns.

Grade	ITF	GTF
10th Kup	Saju Jirugi, Saju Makgi	Saju Jirugi, Saju Makgi
9th Kup	Chon-Ji	Chon-Ji
8th Kup	Dan-Gun	Dan-Gun, Jee-Sang
7th Kup	Do-San	Do-San
6th Kup	Won-Hyo	Won-Hyo, Dhan-Goon
5th Kup	Yul-Gok	Yul-Gok
4th Kup	Joong-Gun	Joong-Gun
3rd Kup	Toi-Gye	Toi-Gye
2nd Kup	Hwa-Rang, Saju-Tulgi	Hwa-Rang
1st Kup	Choong-Moo	Choong-Moo
1st Degree	Kwang-Gae, Po-Eun, Ge-Baek	Kwang-Gae, Po-Eun, Ge-Baek, Jee-Goo
2nd Degree	Eui-Am, Choong-Jang, Ko-Dang <u>or</u> Ju-Che	Eui-Am, Choong-Jang Ko-Dang, Jook-Am
3rd Degree	Sam-Il, Yoo-Sin, Choi-Yong	Sam-Il, Yoo-Sin, Choi-Yong, Pyong-Hwa
4th Degree	Yong-Gae, Ul-Ji, Moon-Moo	Yong-Gae, Ul-Ji, Moon-Moo, Sun-Duk
5th Degree	So-San, Se-Jong	So-San, Se-Jong
6th Degree	Tong-Il	Tong-Il
7th Degree		
8th Degree		

Grade	AIMAA	GM Jhoon Rhee
10th Kup	Chon-Ji	
9th Kup	Dan-Gun	
8th Kup	Do-San	Chon-Ji
7th Kup	Won-Hyo	Dan-Gun
6th Kup	Yul-Gok	Do-San
5th Kup	Joong-Gun	Won-Hyo
4th Kup	Toi-Gye	Yul-Gok
3rd Kup	Hwa-Rang	Joong-Gun
2nd Kup	Choong-Moo	Toi-Gye, Hwa-Rang
1st Kup	Kwang-Gae	Choong-Moo, Chul-Gi*
1st Degree	Po-Eun	Kwang-Gae, Basai*
2nd Degree	Ge-Baek	Po-Eun, Sip-Soo*, Bo-Ichi* or Tonfa-Ichi*
3rd Degree	Yoo-Sin	Ge-Baek, Won-Kan*
4th Degree	Choong-Jang, Ul-Ji	Choi-Yong
5th Degree	Ko-Dang, Sam-Il	* Chul-Gi is Tekki Kata, Basai is Basai-Dai Kata, Sip-Soo is Jitte Kata - all found in Shotokan Karate, Won-Kan is an Okinawan Shorin-Ryu kata and Bo-Ichi/Tonfa-Ichi are Okinawan Kobudo kata's.
6th Degree	Choi-Yong	
7th Degree	Se-Jong	** The above list is based on the forms that Grandmaster Jhoon Rhee taught from 1968 onwards, he has since introduced new forms that he terms 'Martial Arts Ballet' - these are Kyu-Yool, Kumsa, Jayoo, Chosang, Jung-Yee, Pyung -Fa, 'Might for Right' and 'Marriage of East to West' - *unfortunately, all the above are beyond the scope of these books*
8th Degree	Tong-Il	

Kihaps In Patterns

Some, but not all Ch'ang Hon based Taekwon-Do organisations require students to Kihap (Spirit shout) at certain points within the patterns they are performing. The following charts list the various points within the patterns where Kihaps are executed, as detailed by very high ranking and respected Masters within Taekwon-Do and serve as a reference guide for those that practice patterns with Kihaps.

Cross-Referencing

The following charts have been compiled from research and cross-referencing the Kihap points used (or not) by the following Masters of Taekwon-Do:

General Choi, Hong Hi - As the founder of Ch'ang Hon Taekwon-Do and its patterns, research seems to indicate that *'unofficially'* Kihaps were allowed to be performed within the patterns. Despite this the General did not list any Kihap points at all in his books published between 1959 and 1999. Therefore Kihaps were never *'officially'* part of Ch'ang Hon Taekwon-Do or the ITF. It should be noted that, as far as I'm aware, it was always customary to Kihap on completion of a pattern (the last movement), possibly a *'knock on'* effect from Karate. This continued until some time in the early 1980's, when General Choi made it mandatory for those in the ITF to shout the name of the pattern instead of a Kihap, as well as formerly stating that there were to be no more Kihaps executed within the patterns.

Grandmaster Kang, Suh Chong - Originally a student under the Chung Do Kwan under its founder, Grandmaster Lee, Won Kuk and an instructor in the ROK army from 1960 to 1968. Vice president of the ITF from 1977 to 1983. As far as I am aware Grandmaster Kang is still teaching Taekwon-Do in the USA. Grandmaster Kang's Kihap points are referenced from Chon-Ji up to Tong-Il and include both Ko-Dang and Juche.

Grandmaster Kim, Bok Man - A military instructor with the ROK army from 1950 to 1962, Grandmaster Kim obtained the highest non-commissioned officer rank of Sgt. Major. He assisted General Choi in formulating at least 15 of the Ch'ang Hon patterns and further went on to formulate more patterns of his own. These patterns included weapons patterns and he developed his own system of martial art known as *'Chun Kuhn Do'*. Grandmaster Kim's Kihap points are referenced from Chon-Ji, up the 2nd degree patterns and include Ko-dang but not Juche.

Grandmaster Park, Jung Tae - Former ITF Secretary-General and Chairman of the ITF Instruction Committee from 1984 until he left to form the GTF in 1990.

Grandmaster Park played a major role in formulating the pattern *'Juche'* as well as being the main instructor chosen to teach Taekwon-Do in North Korea. He continued to develop his own patterns for the GTF until he passed away in 2002. Grandmaster Park did not teach any Kihap points for the Ch'ang Hon patterns. He has one Kihap point only and it appears in the GTF pattern *'Jook-Am'* (on the 360 degree Reverse Turning Kick). GTF students also shout the name on completion of a pattern, rather than Kihap. Grandmaster Park is an important inclusion in this research due to his former positions within the ITF as well as the fact that he knew and has taught all 25 Ch'ang Hon patterns and didn't teach any Kihaps in them at all.

Grandmaster Rhee, Jhoon Goo - Commonly recognised as the *'Father of American Taekwon-Do'*, he trained at the Chung Do Kwan under Grandmaster Nam, Tae Hi and moved to the USA in 1952. Grandmaster Rhee's Kihap points are referenced from Chon-Ji to Choong-Moo and it is unknown whether he included them in higher grade patterns.

Grandmaster Lim, Won Sup and Grandmaster Lee, Myung Woo - Two pioneering Taekwon-Do instructors who taught in Vietnam. Their combined list was supplied by my good friend Yi, Yun Wook who learned from them while training in Vietnam. Grandmaster Lim (who was part of the ITF until about 1984) replaced Grandmaster Park as the instructor for North Korea) and Grandmaster Lee's combined list references Kihap points from Chon-Ji up to the 1st degree patterns.

Grandmaster Hee, Il Cho - Grandmaster Cho is a well known and respected Taekwon-Do Grandmaster and pioneer. He has authored numerous books and videos on Taekwon-Do, as well as featuring in movies. Grandmaster Cho taught Taekwon-Do to Special Forces soldiers (Korea, India and US) during the 1960's before emigrating to the US in 1968. In the 1980's he was the black belt grading examiner for the TAGB, then in the 1990's he became the Black Belt grading examiner for the GTI. He runs his own organisation (AIMAA) which is respected worldwide. Grandmaster Cho's Kihap points are referenced for the 20 original patterns and do not include Eui-Am, Juche, Moon-Moo, Yon-Gae and So-San.

Grandmaster Choi, Jung Hwa - Grandmaster Choi is the son of the founder of Taekwon-Do (General Choi) and current President of ITF-Canada. He is thought to have helped Grandmaster Park formulate pattern Juche. Though not one of the original Pioneers, Grandmaster Choi is an important figure in Taekwon-Do, however his inclusion in this appendix is even more important as in 2008 he decided to re-introduce Kihaps back into the patterns performed by ITF-C members. Grandmaster Choi's Kihap points are referenced from Chon-Ji up to the 1st degree patterns only because, at the time of writing, the ITF-C has only issued points up to 1st degree, though more have been expected for a while now.

Note: Other ITF groups do not perform these Kihaps, but simply shout the name of the pattern on completion.

Pattern	GM Lim, Won Sup	GM Kim, Bok Man	GM Choi, Jung Hwa (ITF-C)	GM Hee, Il Cho (AIMAA)	GM Jhoon Rhee	GM Kang, Suh Chong
Chon-Ji	#17	#19	#17	#19	#1, #8, #19	#1, #17, #19
Dan-Gun	#8, #17	#8, #21	#8, #17	#8, #17	#1, #8, #21	#1 #8, #17, #19
Do-San	#6	#6, #24	#6, #22	#6, #24	#1, #6, #24	#2, #6, #22, #24
Won-Hyo	#12, #26	#12, #27	#12	#12, #26	#1, #12, #28	#1, #12, #26
Yul-Gok	#27, #36	#21, #36	#24, #27, #36	#24, #36	#21, #36, #38	#0*, #21, #36 #38
Joong-Gun	#12	#12	#12	None	#1, #12, #32	#1, #12, #32
Toi-Gye	#21	#21, #37	#29	#21, #37	#1, #21, #37	#1, #21, #29, #37
Hwa-Rang	#25	#14, #27	#14, #25	#14 & #25	#1, #14, #29	#0*, #12a, #25, #29
Choong-Moo	#9b	#9b, #30	#9b, #19	#9b, #30	#1, #9b, #19, #30	#9a, #12, #19, #32
Kwang-Gae	#31	#23, #27, #35, #39	#23, #27	None	NA	#0*, #12, #31, #39
Po-Eun	#12 & #30	#12 & #30	#12 & #30	None	NA	#1, #18, #36
Ge-Baek	#23, #28	#26, #44	#19, #28	#23, #28	NA	#1, #28, #44

#0* denotes a Kihap placement prior or during the first movement. For Yul-Gok and Hwa-Rang a Kihap is executed prior to the first move of the pattern, for Kwang-Gae a Kihap is performed at the first part of the first movement, when breaking from Heaven Hand with two Knifehand Strikes.

 # a or b denotes a Kihap placement during a move that has one count, but is actually two or more movements, such as the Flying Side Piercing Kick and landing with a Knifehand Guarding Block in Choong-Moo. Please reference the relevant pattern chapters for clarification.

Pattern	GM Lim, Won Sup	GM Kim, Bok Man	GM Choi, Jung Hwa (ITF-C)	GM Hee, Il Cho (AIMAA)	GM Jhoon Rhee	GM Kang, Suh Chong
Ko-Dang	None	#29	NA	None	NA	#27, #37, #39
Eui-Am	None	#45	None	NA	NA	#1, #45
Choong-Jang	None	#8, #50 & #52	None	None	NA	#1, #8, #12, #19, #41, #52
Juche	NA	NA	None	NA	NA	#12b, #24b, #37d, #45
Sam-Il	None	None	None	None	NA	#1, #12, #17b, #33
Yoo-Sin	None	None	None	None	NA	#1, #38, #68
Choi-Yong	None	None	None	None	NA	#1, #46
Yong-Gae	None	None	None	NA	NA	#1, #49
Ul-Ji	None	None	None	None	NA	#1, #6, #12, #17, #27, #33, #42
Moon-Moo	None	None	None	NA	NA	#58,
So-San	None	None	None	NA	NA	#1, #28, #51b, #56b, #72
Se-Jong	None	None	None	None	NA	#1, #7, #21, #24
Tong-Il	None	None	None	None	NA	#17, #19, #38, #56

Research

Further research into the Kihaps points in the Ch'ang Hon tul seems to indicate that rather than being formerly instituted by General Choi himself, the Kihaps used by most instructors are most likely to have been carried forward from previous Karate training and placed within the Ch'ang Hon tul by personal preference and sharing by various Masters. This seems to explain why some Kihaps are in the same place while others are not. I have come to this conclusion due to the discrepancies in their location from Master to Master (which you will see on the lists), as well as information from pioneering masters such as Master CK Choi. If they were *'officially'* instituted by General Choi himself, everyone would be performing them at the same point within each pattern.

Due to the lack of standardization in Taekwon-Do, which didn't occur until the late 1970's/early 80's, this simply carried on until Kihaps were officially removed from the patterns by General Choi once standardisation of the Ch'ang Hon patterns began. However many Masters kept them either because they had left General Choi by then or simply because of personal preference.

To further complicate matters, in interviews with Master George Vitale, Grandmaster CK Choi (who helped design Ge-Baek tul) said that when it was formulated it did not include Kihaps. Grandmaster Park, Jong Soo also has said that General Choi didn't teach Kihaps when instructing patterns. Grandmaster Park lived with General Choi (in his house) in 1965 when General Choi was finalizing his English version of his book and he worked on all the patterns and photographs within the book. Though some instructors did them due to their former karate training, Grandmaster Cho, Sang Min, a 5th dan in 1968 and instructor at the official ITF Instructors course at that time confirmed that Kihaps were used when a pattern finished. This coincides with changing the Kihap at the end to shouting the name of the pattern instead.

If you don't perform Kihaps and wish to know more about them, as well as 'Ki' itself and how it relates to Taekwon-Do there is a fantastic appendix in my first book *(Ch'ang Hon Taekwon-do Hae Sul)* written by my good friend Yi, Yun Wook that goes into a lot of detail about it.

Appendix iv
Sine Wave Study
By Master Paul McPhail, 7th Degree, ITFNZ

This is an analysis of how sine wave is performed in pattern movements in relation to *fast, continuous* and *connecting* motion. This is based on watching General Choi and others perform the movement at various seminars over the years. There seems to be 4 ways of moving from one movement on to the next, as listed below:

Full Sine Wave - This means once the first movement is complete, you then drop your weight down, up, then down again as you complete the next movement (down/up/down).

2/3 Sine Wave - This means completing the first movement, moving straight up then down to complete the next movement (up/down).

1/3 Sine Wave - This means you are already up at the completion of the first movement, so then drop down into the next (down).

Continuous Motion	Moves	Full	2/3	1/3	None
Dan-Gun	13-14 (low block/rising block)	X			
Toi-Gye	7-8 (pressing blk/vertical punch)	X			
Po-Eun	6-12, 24-30 (blocks-punches)		X		
Ge-Baek	5-6 (rising block, low block)	X			
Ge-Baek	37-38 (low guarding blocks)	X			
Eui-Am	5-6, 18-19 (down blk/rising blk)	X			
Sam-Il	30-31 (inward block/punch)	X			
Yoo-Sin	16-17, 18-19 (hook block/punch)		X		
Yoo-Sin	20-21, 25-26 (pressing blk/rising				
Ul-Ji	2-3 (pressing block/rising block)	X			
So-San	52-53, 57-58 (low block/punch)	X			
So-San	71-72 (knifehand guarding blk/	X			

Fast Motion	Moves	Full	2/3	1/3	None
Do-San	15-16, 19-20 (punches)		X		
Yul-Gok	2-3, 5-6 (punches)		X		
Yul-Gok	9-10,13-14 (punches)		X		
Joong-Gun	15-16,18-19 (release/punch)		X		
Hwa-Rang	18-19 (turn-kick/turn-kick/KHGB)	X (block)			X (kicks)
Choong-Moo	14-15 (turn-kick/back-kick)				X
Ge-Baek	3-4 (punches)		X		
Ge-Baek	22-23 (turn-kick/flying side kick)				X
Choong-Jang	46-47 (punches)		X		
Yoo-Sin	2-3 (angle punches)		X		
Yoo-Sin	34-35, 36-37 (dbl forearm/low blk)				X
Choi Yong	21-22 (pressing blocks)		X		
Ul-Ji	11 (X-stance drop)			X	
So-San	5-6, 7-8 (Knifehand Block/punch)		X		
So-San	39-40, 47-48 (punches)		X		
Tong-Il	5-6 (punches)		X		
Tong-Il	14-15 (punches)		X		
Tong-Il	20-21 (punches)		X		

Connecting	Moves	Full	2/3	1/3	None
Yul-Gok	16-17, 19-20 (hooking/punch)			X	
Ge Baek	9-10, 29-30 (scoop/punch)			X	
Yoo-Sin	10-11, 14-15 (scoop block/punch)			X	
Moon-Moo	28-29, 37-38 (scoop block/punch)			X	

It is apparent from studying this chart that there is no direct correlation between the speed of the movement (i.e. fast, continuous or connecting motion) and how the sine wave in the movement is performed.

Thanks to Mr Mark Banicevich, IV Dan, for his assistance with this study.

The True And More Complete History Of Taekwon-Do

By Master George Vitale, 8th Degree

There are many reasons why the history of Tae Kwon Do is so confusing and has often been so distorted. First and foremost is the problem of having the same name of Tae Kwon Do applied to different activities. Is Tae Kwon Do a martial art or a martial sport, both or somewhere in between? Was Tae Kwon Do developed in the Korean military for self defense or in the civilian arena to be a national sport, or some combination thereof? Am I confusing you even more yet? Do not worry, hang in there and read on. Hopefully it will get clearer if you remain open minded to what happened, when it happened and who made it happen. These are the easy aspects of Tae Kwon Do's history, and they are fairly straight forward. The why is often more complicated. However understanding the context of the times when it all took place should even help the understanding of the opinion based why.

We know from the study of history not connected to Tae Kwon Do that Korea suffered under a long and brutal occupation by the colonial power of Imperial Japan. This period covered the start of the 20th Century and lasted till August 15, 1945, when Japan surrendered ending World War II. During this time span the Korean language was outlawed. Schools were forced to abandon Korean subjects, including history and were teaching Japanese in place, to attempt the further subjugation of the Korean people. Koreans were forced to take Japanese names. Korean males were conscripted into the Japanese military compelled to fight for Japan. Korean females were turned into comfort women (prostitutes) for the Japanese soldiers. There was a far reaching attempt to eradicate Korean culture and history with the goal of making Koreans Japanese. In effect the proud and distinct sovereign people, culture and Nation of Korea were being absorbed into the expanding Japanese Empire.

President Syngman Rhee

Understanding this is so very critical to understanding post World War II Korea. After being so beaten down and humiliated by this foreign colonial grasp for power, Koreans were more than eager to reconnect with their proud culture and history. There was a national movement to reinvigorate Korean pride. According to noted historian and Korean Martial Arts Grandmaster Dr. He Young Kimm, PhD and his book on the "History of Korea and Hapkido" (2008) the first President of The Republic of (south) Korea Rhee Seung Man, who took office in 1948, had a strict anti-Japanese policy. This in effect made it against the law to promote or embrace anything Japanese.

Readers and students of Tae Kwon Do must also understand clearly that Korea back in the middle of the 20th Century was not the affluent economic giant that it is today in the 21st Century. In fact the United States Department of State's website on April 15, 2010 lists The Republic of Korea as the world's 13th largest economy. The Republic of Korea's Embassy in Washington DC states that they are a Member of the G20 and will host the next meeting of the world's 20th largest economies. It was a very poor developing country when Tae Kwon Do was just starting out. In addition it was ravaged by a devastating civil war that not only killed millions but destroyed approximately 80% of the peninsular. Telephones did not come into use until the early 1960s. What is also a very critical point to grasp is that there was not the number of martial arts schools that seem to be on every corner, back in Korea at that time. In fact, the martial arts in general in those days were not like they were today.

Mr. Michael Rosenbaum in his book The Fighting Arts: Their Evolution from Secret Societies to Modern Times (2002) points out that the martial arts in times long past were related for the most part to the military. They revolved and evolved around the weapons of the day. As weaponry became more advanced, less emphasis naturally had to be placed on fighting with the body. Basically the development went from early forms of hand to hand combat, to that of weapons, like sticks, clubs, knives and spears. Once the advent of gunpowder was applied to the making of guns, single shot pistols evolved into rifles, revolvers, semi automatic, automatic machine guns and cannons. As technology advanced, it was of course applied to weapons as well, resulting in tanks, jet fighters, submarines and weapons of mass destruction. Likewise at these innovations took hold and were applied to the military, the martial arts training warriors or soldiers received adapted as well.

On the civilian side an evolution took place as well. The practice of the martial arts in the past was not like it is today. It was not as organized and as widespread as we now see it. There was a fighter who shared what he knew with friends and family. Often on such a limited basis that according to Mr. Neil Horton in his book Japanese Martial Arts (2005) they had only one or a couple of students at a time. Nor were the training methods categorized and documented as they are today. It can be assumed that the transmission of knowledge was for the most part verbally. This small circle was then entrusted with passing on this system. In fact Horton states they "taught in isolation from the outside world and restricted to the eyes of the extended family".

As societies progressed, so did the emphasis or reasons for civilian practice of the martial arts change. The martial arts started to add a component of sport to it. Jigoro Kano, the oft recognized founder of Judo is reported to have even introduced a belt system. Master Gichin Funakoshi, who many refer to as the Father of Karate and founder of Shotokan took his martial art from Okinawa to Japan. It was here in Japan that it was taught in the academic school system. It has been said that this version had more of a sports element to it.

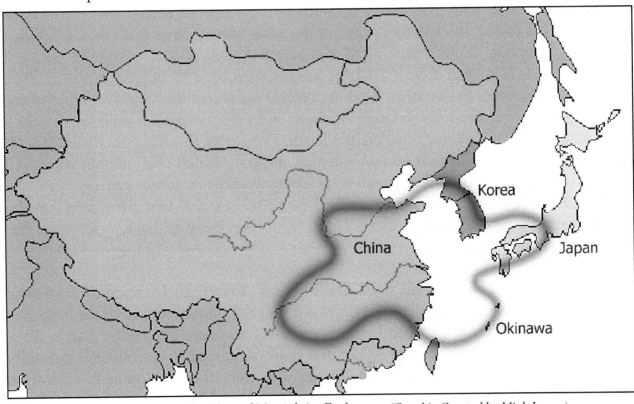

Asia Map Showing the Flow of Martial Art Exchanges (Graphic Created by Minh Luong)

So what then was going on in Korea around this time? For the most part as far as the practice of the martial arts goes, nothing much was really taking place. Please remember that the martial arts craze had not become widespread and did not yet reach Western society. Of course the West had their own systems of fighting that evolved as well. However the phenomenon of traditional Asian martial arts with the concept of the Dao or Do was simply not that common in the 1800s. We know this from many sources including but not limited to the Education Ministry of The Republic of Korea, the official Kukkiwon Textbook (2006) published by the World Taekwondo Headquarters (Kukkiwon), a book published by the Ministry of Culture and Tourism of The Republic of Korea in 2000 titled "Taekwondo: The Spirit Of Korea" and the World Taekwondo Federation's own website as of March 30, 2010:

"In the modern times of Korea, the Chosun dynasty [1392-1910] the imperial Korea and the Japanese colonial rule until 1945, Taekwondo was rather called "subakhui" than "Taekkyon" and it suffered an eventual loss of official support from the central government as the weapons were modernized for national defense, although the subkhui was still popular in the early days of Chosun".

"The Chosun dynasty was founded on the ideology of Confucianism, which resulted in rejecting Buddhism and giving more importance on literary art than martial art. Nonetheless, the Annals of Chosun Dynasty tells about the contests of subakhui

ordered by local officials for the purpose of selecting soldiers and others ordered by the kings who enjoyed watching subakhui contests at the times of feasts. It was also ruled by the defense department that a soldier should be employed when he wins three other contestants in the subakhui bouts. However, as the government progressed, the government officials began to lay more importance on power struggles than on the interest of defense, naturally neglecting promotion of martial arts ".

"Then, it was only in the days of King Jungjo after the disgraceful invasion of Korea by the Japanese [1592] that the royal government revived strong defense measures by strengthening military training and martial art practice. Around this period there was a publication of the so-called "Muyedobo-Tongji," a book of martial art illustrations, which 4th volume entitled "hand-fighting techniques" contained the illustration of 38 motions, exactly resembling today's Taekwondo poomsae and basic movements, although those motions cannot be compared with today's Taekwondo poomsae, which has been modernized through scientific studies".

"However, the Japanese colonial government totally prohibited all folkloric games including Taekkyon in the process of suppressing the Korean people. The martial art Taekkyon [Taekwondo] had been secretly handed down only by the masters of the art until the liberation of the country in 1945. Song Duk-Ki, one of the then masters testifies that his master was Im Ho who was reputed for his excellent skills of Taekkyon, "jumping over the walls and running through the wood just like a tiger." (explanation of taekkon techniques in muyedobo-tongji (general illustrations of techniques) (scene of contest) ".

The Ministry of Culture describes the historical background of Taekwondo by stating that during the Chosun Dynasty "unarmed martial arts suffered greatly from the heavy emphasis of the ruling class on the literary over physical activities". It goes on to point out that Su Bak Hi was a form of folk game, with Hi meaning play or game. It explains how this was kept alive and eventually was possibly renamed or came to be known as Taek Kyon. This publication points to works by an American Anthropologist by the name of Stewart Culin. In his book "Korean Games" (1895), which I have a copy of and have consulted, the Culture Ministry refers to a picture of "two children engaging in a teakkyon match". They add the sport became so popular that people bet on the outcome of the matches, prompting the conservative neo-Confucian government to ban this "inappropriate activity". This seemed to have lead to "its gradual disappearance from common culture".

The 2006 Kukkiwon Textbook repeats almost verbatim the text reprinted above that was downloaded from the WTF website. In fact many if not all WTF or Kukki Taekwondo books that have been published and contain a history section follow this general template. Why? What does this mean? How come this pattern exists? Well a simple answer would be, once something is stated, it gets repeated and often comes

Portraits of the 3 Kukkiwon Presidents - (L to R) Dr. Kim Un Yong, Uhm Won Kyu and Lee Seung Wan

to be accepted, even though it has little connection to truth of where Tae Kwon Do actually came from. The more complete answer however is that it has taken on a life of its own to cover the connection that Tae Kwon Do has to karate. It was done for nationalist reasons of Korea, who suffered tremendously under the brutal hand of Imperial Japan, when they occupied Korea and tried to destroy Korean culture, history and their unique identity as a proud people.

This fabrication is not limited to the WTF side of Taekwondo. The International Taekwon-Do Federation (ITF) and Gen. Choi Hong Hi were guilty of much the same acts. However Gen. Choi always made clear the karate training he received while living in Japan. He also painted a glowing picture of Korean martial arts of the past, the Hwa Rang Warriors, Taek Kyon, etc. and how they influenced his Taekwon-Do. However in later years he cut back on stories of his own Taek Kyon training, saying it was limited, not much at all and then finally saying that he was told stories of it by his calligraphy teacher. This can be seen from reviewing his written works and interviews he gave over the years to such people as the legendary American martial artist Bob Wall and historian Dr. He Young Kimm.

General Choi at 33 years of age and 1 Star Brigadier General

We should not take seriously claims that Tae kwon Do is 2,000 years old, as that is an orchestrated myth. However that does not mean that Korea did not have its own fighting systems in place long ago, as it is as certain as can be that they did. All locations around the world had some sort of indigenous fighting styles that were put in place for protection. This goes without saying that Korea also had their own martial arts. So we can all pretty much concede this point, while not confusing this accepted conclusion with the fabrication that Tae Kwon Do is 2,000 years old or has a verifiable direct connection to those physical activities long since gone.

When we refer to the often quoted book from the 1790s that was commissioned by then King Jung Jo in 1789 when he directed Generals Yi Duk Mu, Pak Dong Su and Park Je Ga to compile the martial arts of the time, we see how silly it is to try to make a connection to the Korean martial arts of the past to Tae Kwon Do. This book is titled Muye Dobo Tongji: The Comprehensive Illustrated Manual of Martial Arts of Ancient Korea. Now the reader does not have to rely on my interpretation that this connection is laughable, for they can get a copy as I did of the English translation completed in 2000 by Dr. Sang H. Kim, PhD.

If one takes the time to review this work, they will see that the four volumes are about military tactics, weapons, shields and using these arms on horseback, along with horseback riding techniques. Are there any martial arts or hand to hand combat contained within this set of works? Yes, there are 16 pages on Kwon Bup, often associated with Chinese martial arts, which translates to fist method. When one sees for themselves the basic figure drawings and limited text, they too will ask where the connection to today's Tae Kwon Do is! To get further evidence of this assertion please review John A. Della Pia's article in the Journal of Asian Martial Arts (1994). One can also read an article by Oerjan Nilsen, a self described Kukki/WTF black belt instructor in the April 2009 issue Totally TKD, an on-line Tae Kwon Do magazine. Mr. Nilsen also studied Tae Kwon Do at Chosun University in Kwang Ju Korea for a year from 2007 to 2008.

So if Tae Kwon Do is not 2,000 years old and does not have a direct verifiable connection to Korean martial arts of the past, where did it actually come from? Why does it seem to be that official sources appear to be so misleading? When we examine the why, the where does it come from question becomes easier to answer.

Grandmaster Lee Chong Woo. Possibly the Most Important Kukki TKD Master

According to Grandmaster Lee Chong Woo in a 2002 interview conducted by Yook Sung Chul that appeared in a Korean magazine named Shin Dong A he was the one who came up with the story as they had nothing much else to offer in those early days when they started to spread Taekwondo around. When asked directly if the schools that opened up after the end of the occupation taught karate Grandmaster Lee replied "The basic movements, such as the blocking and hitting techniques, were identical with Karate." The reporter Mr. Yook then asked: *Is Karate the only martial art that had an impact on Taekwondo in the process of its creation after Liberation? No other influences at all?*

Grandmaster Chong Woo Lee's response was: "That is a candid statement. I am the one who wrote books bringing in various materials of all sorts, but now is the time to disclose the facts. All the masters who taught Karate got together and formulated basic Taekwondo forms, and I took a central role. It should not be a big issue now to disclose this fact, because we are at the top of the world."

Grandmaster Lee Chong Woo who was a leading member of the Jidokwan, playing a significant role in reorganizing this powerful and influential Kwan after their founder and teacher disappeared during the Korean War. He was probably the most pivotal 2nd generation Korean martial arts leader who developed much of the rules that eventually became Olympic sport Taekwondo. He was a critical member who formed the Korean Tae Soo Do Association in 1961. He went on to help Gen. Choi form the ITF and was their first director of technique. He served in many capacities in the KTA, serving as vice president of both the Kukkiwon and WTF. Grandmaster Lee also was on the committee that created the Taeguek Poomsae. As we can see from his own words, he played an important part in initially hiding the connection Taekwondo has to karate. He finally has come on record stating the truth.

Additional significant leaders of Taekwondo have challenged the fabrication as well. A textbook published by the Korean Minister of Education in 1976 serves as a guide of what has become the standard repeated template that has been repeated all too often. According to Dr. Steven Capener, PhD, a Kukki Taekwondo black belt and former employee of the WTF that teaches in Korean Universities, says the "typical writings regarding Taekwondo history which begins with two pages dealing with the probable need and origin of fighting skills in prehistoric, tribal Korea. Next are about 20 pages dealing with the sonbae of Koguryo and the hwarang of Shilla and their practice of Taekwondo which was then called subak or Taekkyon. Following are five pages regarding the subakhui of the Koryo dynasty. Then five pages regarding the Taekkyon of the Choson dynasty, and, finally, two sentences dealing with the fortunes of Taekwondo in the period from the end of the 19th century until the liberation of Korea from Japanese colonial rule in 1945.

A review of the available literature shows this to be a typical pattern. From an academic point of view, however, this seems an illogical treatment of the history. Much more effort is devoted to attempting to demonstrate that some sort of unarmed fighting form existed in Korea during a period in which there is little or no written historical documentation, while practically no attention is given to the period in which Taekwondo actually began to appear in its modern form in Korea, and for which there is much more historical evidence".

Olympic Champion Herb Perez from the United States who has also won numerous national gold medals is a WTF official and active on the national level as well. Mr. Perez, a lawyer has played a part of significance in many areas of Taekwondo. He has collaborated with Dr. Capener on such research into the true history of

Taekwondo. Grandmaster Kim Soo was a foreign correspondent for Black Belt magazine in the 1960s when he was still living in Korea. In a 2006 interview conducted by Robert McLain he stated "because of the Japanese occupation of Korea from 1909 to 1945, the second generation of martial artists hated the Japanese. Connection with anything Japanese, karate for example, was frowned upon. Even though karate was from Okinawa, most kwan founders studied karate taught in Japan during college".

When we examine what happened and the circumstances that it took place in, we can see more clearly the reason why the history has been manipulated and hidden. Korea is a proud nation with a long history of a distinct language and culture. The suffering that they withstood under the brutal occupation as a colony of Imperial Japan helps us to see why they wished to hide the connection to karate. Today young scholars and present generation writers like Doug Cook, a Kukki Taekwondo master and Simon John O'Neill who authored a book on the Taeguek Poomsae, along with others are now telling more of the complete history of Tae kwon Do. These authors, an American and European respectfully do not have the biases, nor do they face some of the pressure that earlier Korean writers faced with keeping the truth from being more fully discussed or disclosed.

Likewise both myself, an American and Mr. Stuart Anslow, a European, we strive very carefully to not put forth biased information and are set on helping the readers and students of Tae Kwon Do understand the more full and complete history of the Art we love so much. As such, we now move into the section that tells of the seven Korean men who went abroad to live. While living outside of Korea, they also became exposed to the martial arts.

Master Vitale with Several Korean TKD Pioneers & GMs Lim, McNeely and Dr. Mencia

RO BYUNG JIK founded the Song Moo Kwan, the School of the Pine Tree. Some records indicate he first taught at the Kwan Duk Jung Archery School in KaeSung starting on March 11, 1944. He was forced to close a few months later as Korea was still occupied by Japan. Scott Shaw reports that he reopened on May 2, 1946 in Dong Hung Dong KaeSung. After the Korea War ended the Song Moo Kwan relocated to Ah Hyung Dong Map Gu district of Seoul and was established on September 20, 1953. Grandmaster Ro studied Shotokan Karate under Gichin Funakoshi while living in Japan. He served as a vice president of the 1959 Korean Tae Kwon Do Association and later as the 4th president of the Korean Taekwon-Do Association. In 2010 Grandmaster Ro was approaching his 91st birthday, making him the oldest Korean martial artist known to be still alive. He is now living in the USA.

GM Byung Jik Ro
Song Moo kwan Founder

GM Lee Won Kuk Chung Do Kwan Founder and Gen Choi co-founder of Oh Do Kwan, who succeeded GM Lee as honorary head of the Chung Do Kwan after he left for Japan

LEE WON GUK founded the Chung Do Kwan meaning School of the Blue Wave during the occupation period in September of 1944 at the Yong Shin School in Suh Dae Moon Gu section of Seoul. After WWII ended he forged a relationship with local officials teaching so many police officers that his gym became known as the National Police Headquarters DoJang. In 1926 He went to study at a college in Japan. There Grandmaster Lee also studied under the Father of Modern Karate Sensei Gichin Funakoshi along with Grandmaster Ro Byung Jik, who later founded the Song Moo Kwan. According to Scott Shaw he started his martial arts training at age 19. Some of his very influential students were now grandmasters Kang Suh Chong, Son Duk Sung, Uhm Won Gyu, Hyun Jong Myun, Nam Tae Hi, Paek Joon Ji, Han Cha Kyo & Jhoon Rhee. These students would later become some of the major leaders of making Tae Kwon Do into the art or sport it is today.

CHUN SANG SUP founded the School of Martial Training and called it the Chosun Yun Moo Kwan Kong Soo Do Bu on May 3, 1946 in Seoul Korea. Scott Shaw says that Grandmaster Chun may have taught privately in Korea during the occupation period as early as 1940. He learned Japanese Shotokan Karate. He was later disappeared to north Korea during the Korean War. It is not known

GM Chun Sang Sup Founder of Choson Yun Moo Kwan Kong Soo Do Bu

if he was killed, defected or was kidnapped. A very influential student, Grandmaster Lee Chong Woo along with Dr. Yoon Bwe Byung changed the name at this time to the Ji Do Kwan. This Kwan was instrumental in devising many of the Olympic TKD rules.

GM Hwang Kee
Moo Duk Kwan Founder

HWANG KEE founded the Moo Do Kwan or the School of Martial Virtue circa 1946 at the Yong San train station in Seoul. As a result its nickname became the Railroad DoJang. He reports learning about Taek Kyon when he lived in northern Korea by the border with China. This could have been from watching a neighbor train from a distance when he was 7 years of age. Living in Manchuria he learned Chinese martial arts and claims to have studied a form of karate there as well as also studying it from a book. Grandmaster Hwang Kee served as the Chief Director of the 1959 Korean Taekwon-Do Association. He formed the Korean Su Bak Do Association in 1960 and authored several books. His research with the Muye Dobo Tonji resulted in him establishing Su Bak Do, supposedly linking this art to Korea's past. This focus moved him from the Tae Kwon Do unification efforts.

YOON BYUNG IN founded the YMCA Kwon Bup Bu which translates as School of the Fist Method in Jong Ro Seoul in 1946. He studied Chinese martial arts, including Joo An Pa in Manchuria. While living in Japan he reportedly studied Karate under Shudokan founder Toyama Kanken. During the Korean War he was taken to north Korea where he eventually taught the martial art they called Kuk Sul. Robert McLain reports during the Korean War massive bombings destroyed the YMCA building in late 1950, early 1951. In 1952 an early influential student Grandmaster Nam Lee Suk changed the name to the Chang Moo Kwan after relocating the Dojang to a Postal Administration Department Club.

1948 Photo of GM Yoon Byung In Founder of YMCA Kwon Bup Bu (Chang Moo Kwan)

YOON KWE BYUNG according to Grandmaster Kim Soo was the chief master at Han MuKwan in Tokyo in 1947 which had ties to Grandmaster Kanken Toyama's Shutokan. He also studied under Grandmaster Kanken Toyama and under Mabun Kenwa the founder of Shito-Ryu. Various reports have Dr. Yoon achieving the rank of 4th or 5th degree, which was a great accomplishment in those days. Dr. He Young Kimm has described him as a karate man that actually earned a 7th degree,

Dr. Yoon Kwe Byung, Ji Do Kwan 2nd Kwan Jang Nim

the highest of any Korean during this time period. In the Modern History of Tae Kwon Do the authors Kang and Lee credit Dr. Yoon with coming up with the compromise name of Tae Soo Do, although he preferred the karate name of Kong Soo Do, when he saw the negotiations would never agree on either Tae Kwon Do, Kong Soo Do or Tang Soo Do. He did not continue with the Taekwondo unification efforts, preferring to stay karate and work with Grandmaster Hwang Kee and Subakdo.

Rare photo of Major-General Choi in 2 Star Dress Uniform

CHOI HONG HI founded the Oh Do Kwan which means the gym of my way along with Col. Nam Tae Hi in 1954. Gen. Choi reports that he had been teaching since 1946. Kang and Lee in a Modern History of Tae Kwon Do state that Col. Nam taught in the Army since 1947. As a teenager Gen. Choi says he was introduced to Taek Kyon and studied karate in Japan. He came up with the name Tae Kwon Do and served as vice president of the Tae Kwon Do Association of Korea in 1957. He then founded the Korean Taekwon-Do Association in 1959 and the International Taekwon-Do Federation in 1966. When Ambassador Choi returned from his diplomatic assignment in Malaysia, where he introduced Taekwon-Do there, he was elected the 3rd president of the Korean Tae Soo Do Association and was able to have the name changed back to Taekwon-Do.

Gen. Choi was the author of several books on Taekwon-Do from 1959 to 1999, including the first ever. He led the 1st Taekwon-Do demonstrations abroad in 1959 & the Goodwill world tour in 1965.

These seven men listed above studied for the most part karate and six of the seven studied it in Japan. There was some Chinese influence as well, with both Grandmasters Hwang Kee and Yoon Byung In making the claim to have studied Chinese martial arts in Manchuria, a part of China, in addition to karate. Some energy has been expended to say that karate is from Okinawa, so it is not Japanese. While this may be true, the fact remains that the six Koreans did learn karate in Japan. Others will add that all of these countries are part of Asia and much of their culture is shared. There is also truth to this statement.

The fact remains however that these Korean men opened up or taught at Korean karate schools back in Korea. This instruction included the use of karate Gis, karate katas as well as a belt system that was taken from Japanese karate and judo. During the occupation period the martial arts that were around according to Dr. Kimm He Young were judo, kendo and archery. In an interview with Dr. Kim Un Yong, the first president of the WTF, he stated to me that kendo, judo and sumo were allowed. So we have the fact that martial arts fell out of favor in Korea pre occupation period.

Then they were outlawed during the occupation by the Japanese. So it becomes clear to see that when World War II ended, the schools that did open up had no real and direct connection to Korean martial arts of a time period that had long passed.

Korean Human Cultural Asset Taek Kyon Master Song Duk Ki

Literature boasts of a connection to Taek Kyon. This connection is so important to Korea, that a Taek Kon master by the name of Son Duk Ki was named as a human cultural asset along with Shin Han Seung by the Korean government on June 1, 1983. In addition, Taek Kyon itself is designated as an intangible Korean cultural asset #76 as well. This according to Robert Young in his Journal of Asian Martial Arts article (1993) is the only Korean martial art to ever receive this distinction. However Master Son Duk Ki stated that he was not able to find anyone to train with after the occupation ended, nor was he consulted by any Tae Kwon Do leaders. Associations that were formed as a result of his work deny any connection to Tae Kwon Do. This is confirmed by Young's work and that conducted by Yung Ouyang (Journal of Asian Martial Arts, 1997).

Second generation Tae Kwon Do leaders like Grandmaster Lee Chong Woo downplay any connection to Taek Kyon. So while Taek Kyon could have been some sort of Korean martial art, it apparently was more of a Korean folk game that had all but disappeared for some time in Korea, making it of little relevance to Tae Kwon Do. Dr. Steve Capener in his research even goes on to say that it was something that was further limited to the Seoul area, using that to even discount stories of Gen. Choi's exposure to it. Taek Kyon leaders Chung Kyeong Hwa and Lee Yong Bok could not come up with any evidence to support these claims as well (Young, 1993).

So we clearly see that while Korea probably had some type of systemized fighting long ago, there is no verifiable connection to Tae kwon Do. The folk game of Taek Kyon played little if any part in Tae Kwon Do's development. The seven Koreans who studied karate abroad and were the first generation leaders, were for the most part still teaching karate in Korea when they returned home. What part if any did they play in Tae Kwon Do's development and propagation?

Founders Chun Sang Sup and Yoon Byung In disappeared during the Korean War which started June 1950 and ended in July of 1953. Kang Won Sik, formerly of the Korean Taekwondo Association (KTA) and Lee Kyong Myong formerly of the WTF in their work A Modern History of Taekwondo (1999) report that Grandmasters Chun and Yoon opened their Kwans in 1946. This gave them approximately 4 years of being on the development scene in Korea before the chaos of the war ensued. During the devastating war, both were reported missing. Hence we can see that there involvement was somewhat limited.

Likewise the founder of the Chung Do Kwan, Lee Won Kuk fled to Japan to escape political oppression by the presidential administration of Seung Man Rhee. Mr. Rhee was an anti-communist with deep feelings of anti-Japanese sentiment as he lived abroad for much of his life due to the brutal occupation that the Japanese Empire afflicted upon Korea. There were rumors of Grandmaster Lee having some pro-Japanese leanings. As a result he was

Early Chung Do Kwan Photo
with GM Kang Suh Chong , one of the Most Senior Members

arrested and beaten by authorities. He moved to Japan around the outbreak of the Korean War. This would have only allowed him to play a part in the formation for just 6 years.

Founder Hwang Kee was involved in several attempts to unite the Korean martial arts during the years from the early days of the formative years up until 1965. These early attempts were uniting under karate using names like Tang Su Do or Kong Su Do, to avoid the obvious Japanese leanings. His agreements to unite were usually short lived. He focused on forming his own Tang Soo Do Association in the 1950s. Then later on he settled on the Su Bak Do Association, never again working with the other Kwan leaders to unite.

Grandmaster Ro Byung Jik was the only original Kwan founder who played a part in unification efforts from the onset in the 1940s, till the successful attempts that started to bear fruit in the late 1960s. As such, the founder of the Song Moo Kwan should receive credit for his work towards this goal over the years. These efforts began when he and three of the other original Kwan founders, Lee, Yoon and Chun tried to unite in some fashion around the late 1940s, but were not successful.

During the Korean War the Kwans were forced to close and with their members fleeing south. Grandmaster Ro again worked towards a unification of some sort. This time another Korean who studied karate in Japan played a part. He was of course Dr. Yoon Kwe Byung. However the rest of the participants were the second generation leaders who stepped up to take the place of their teachers who were either no longer alive or living in south Korea. This next generation consisted of Son Duk Sung, Lee Chong Woo, Hyun Jong Myun, Jo Young Joo, Lee Nam Suk and Kim In Hwa. They succeeded in forming the Korean Kong Soo Do Association. In less than a month

Grandmaster Hwang Kee withdrew after a disagreement over testing procedures. He looked then to form his own Tang Soo Do Association. Grandmaster Ro was the Chief Director of this Association.

As more Kwans opened as off shoots or breakaways from the original five Kwans, more names were applied to the Korean karate that they were still for the most part doing. Of course some Koreanization was going on in individual ways to start making what they were doing less related to their

Taekwon-Do Naming Committee, led by General Choi who named the art - Tae Kwon Do

common Japanese karate roots. The martial arts were called Kong Soo Do, Tang Soo Do, Kwon Bup and now Su Bak Do and Hwa Soo Do. At this time a young general in the Republic of (south) Korean Army came on the scene. His name was Choi Hong Hi and he co-founded the Oh Do Kwan in 1954 with a young and then Lieutenant Nam Tae Hi. He had been teaching Tang Soo Do in the Army since 1946, while Nam had been teaching there since 1947. Gen. Choi, because of the power he yielded being a founding member of the Korean Military and an Army General in a poor and developing Korea, was able to use his influence to summon a committee to find a unification name for their developing Korean martial arts.

Gen. Choi submitted the name Tae Kwon Do to the board which consisted of not only other martial artists, like Son Duk Sung and Hyun Jong Myun, but prominent leaders of Korean society such as elected politicians, other military generals, businessmen and newsmen. The name was approved and April 11, 1955 is the date associated with the naming of Tae Kwon Do. Gen. Choi eventually secured the approval of President Seung Man Rhee, when he was able to get President Rhee to write Tae Kwon Do in calligraphy using Chinese characters. While the name was apparently offered as an umbrella term, few adopted

Republic of Korea 1st President Rhee, Seung Man's Taekwon-Do Caligraphy in Chinese, 1955. Proving TKD name accepted by Korean Govt.

it. Its use was limited to Gen. Choi, his soldiers at the Oh Do Kwan and those in the civilian gym, Chung Do Kwan that were loyal to him. To solidify the use of the name he had the signs of these 2 Kwans changed from Tang Soo Do to Tae Kwon Do. He also ordered the soldiers to shout Tae Kwon when saluting in training.

Although the Oh Do Kwan was not an original Kwan the Korean Amateur Sports Association mediator Lee In Tai, a senior member of their Board of Directors found that since Gen. Choi had trained thousands of soldiers in order to teach Tae Kwon Do to the Army it deserved to be on par. This decision was handed down after leaders of the five original Kwans protested that the Oh Do Kwan should not be included in unification talks in the 1950s. They asserted that this Kwan was not established prior to the Korean War, nor was it a charter member of the Korean Kong Soo Do association or Korean Tang Su Doo Association. Noted historian and Korean Martial Artist Dr. He Young Kimm documented this in the history section of his book on Tae Kwon Do.

The finding of the Korean Amateur Sports Association paved the way for Gen. Choi and the Oh Do Kwan to take part in the discussions which led to the formation of the Korean Taekwon-Do Association in 1959. Gen. Choi was the first president, with Grandmaster Ro Byung Jik serving as the vice president. Few if any can legitimately deny the role that the Korean Army under Gen. Choi played in the development of Taekwon-Do as a martial art. Nor can we ignore the thousands of soldiers that were exposed to his Chang Hon system as military service was mandatory for all Korean males. Some of these soldiers and officers became the next generation Taekwon-Do leaders who spread this art around the world.

WTF Award Presented to Col. Nam Tae Hi on the 44th Anniversary of the ITF

Now what were these soldiers training in, what were they developing and how were they developing it? Well in the beginning it was basically the same karate that they were doing in the civilian Kwans. The chief instructor was Col. Nam Tae Hi and his assistant was Sgt. Han Cha Kyo. Both of these men were early members of the Chung Do Kwan. In fact it was the Chung Do Kwan members that played an important early role in the Oh Do Kwan. These early instructors were Gen. Choi, Major Kim Suk Kyu, Col. Ko Jae Chun, Gen. Woo Jong Lim, Col. Baek Joon Ki, Lt. Col. Lee Sang Ku, Kim Jong Chan and Hyun Jong Myung. All of these men with the exception of Gen. Woo and Kim Jing Chan had verifiable links to the Chung Do Kwan. There was even a claim that Gen. Choi trained at the Chung Do Kwan for a time as well. Regardless of that, he was exerting influence over it for a time as the honorary head.

The first changes that took place were with the new Korean patterns that were created starting in 1955 with Hwa Rang Tul. This pattern was the first Korean one created and was designed primarily by Col. Nam and his assistant Sgt. Han under the direction of Gen. Choi. Col. Nam then played the major role of designing Chung Mu Tul along with Gen. Choi. Sgt. Han then was the primary creator of Ul Ji Tul assisting Gen. Choi in formulating this pattern.

Grandmaster Choi Chang Keun, a soldier himself who assisted Gen. Choi with creating Gae Baek Tul in 1961 described the process in a series of talks and interviews that I have had with him over the years as such: Gen. Choi would have certain details in his head, like the pattern diagram, number of movements and the name of the Korean patriot or historical event that the pattern would be named after. He then would have us work out the various movements with him as he directed and we acted. He then would ask us what we thought about the sequence and the like, such as how did the movements feel and fit together or flow. We then of course gave him the appropriate feedback, as we continued to fine tune the patterns.

In an interview conducted by Master Earl Weiss that appeared in the September 2000 issue of Taekwondo Times Magazine Col. Nam stated that "he performed the physical part of the new patterns as General Choi was mapping them out. He made an analogy saying that it was as if General Choi wrote the script and was the director, and he was the actor". Mr. Philip Hawkins who has done such brilliant work interviewing many original Pioneers of Taekwon-Do elicited a similar response from

Gen Choi Col Nam and GM Kang Yon Ho, one of the Most Senior TKD Masters 7th Dan in 1968 stated he contributed 2 Step Sparring and the Color Yellow belt to the grading

Grandmaster Lee Yoo Sun in an interview that appeared in the July 2009 issue of Totally TKD. Grandmaster Lee recalls memories of standing in front of Gen. Choi as he sat behind his desk calling out pattern movements. "He would call out Lee, knife hand guarding block, forward front punch and so on. Sometimes he would get annoyed and would say Lee get out! And I would leave until I was called back in again".

The movement away from the very evident karate roots by the military Taekwon-Do men was at first the patterns. Gen. Choi a fervent patriot was determined to spread Korean history and culture through his Taekwon-Do patterns. He named them after great Korean patriots or significant events or concepts in Korean history or culture. This was part of his nationalist fervor. He was set on protecting Korean identity through his Taekwon-Do by insuring parts of it were spread worldwide helping to insure that it would never be eradicated again, if Korea was ever oppressed or occupied by an invading force.

In a 1999 interview conducted by Maria Heron for the Times, a United Kingdom publication he was asked how did the patterns come about? His answer is most instructive: "When the Japanese invaded Korea they tried to remove the Korean nationality. You could not go to school and be educated if you were not Japanese. I was left a man with no country and therefore no national pride". "The Patterns of Taekwon-Do represent the history of Korea from time in legend to this century. The propagation of Taekwon-Do throughout the world has also enabled, through the patterns, a small part of Korean history to be learned by its practitioners. A part of Korea therefore now exists across the whole world and Korea's nationality and history can never be removed by oppressors again".

While these patterns were the start of the movement away from karate, they were initially performed with very "karate like" movements. Numerous accounts even say that these new patterns were just re-arranged movements from the earlier karate katas. The same critiques have been made about the Palgwe forms and Taeguek poomsae that were devised in the mid 1960s and early 1970s respectively. According to Ian Abernethy and John Hancock and others, these earlier katas were first called Pinan, Chinese for safe from harm. When Gichin Funakoshi, often called the father of modern karate moved from Okinawa to introduce his Shotokan karate style to mainland Japan, he changed the name to a more Japanese friendly term Heian, which means peaceful mind. When those seven Korean men listed above studied karate abroad, they returned with these katas. However they used the term Pyong Ahn, which is the Korean pronunciation for the Chinese term Pinan. Of course the Koreans would not use the Japanese term Heian.

In the Korean karate schools that opened when the occupation was ending, they did these karate katas, even though they used the Korean name. This was the start of making their martial art more Korean centered. Gen. Choi took this a major step further by creating new Korean patterns along with his soldiers under his command in the Korean Army. Naming them after Korean historical figures and concepts helped instill national pride. Over the passage of time, he required his students and followers to do them different from the karate movements. This evolution occurred over time. At first he wanted them to move more in an up down motion, instead of the trademark karate "hip twist".

This vertical movement of the hips is documented as early as the mid 1960s. In an interview with Grandmaster Kim Young Soo, the chief instructor of the ITF instructors' course in Seoul, Philip Hawkins reports in the July 2005 issue of TKD and the Korean Martial Arts, that they called it at the time knee spring. Grandmaster

CK Choi has called it natural motion in my exchanges with him. While the degree of the vertical movement has changed over the years, as did the later emphasis on an initial down or relax first before the rise, this was the start of making some physical differences from the karate like movements. If one views a latter day You Tube video of an ITF Tul and compare the "bouncy" movement with the audible breathing, one can not help but see the similarity to the flowing up down movements with Taek Kyon. Other aspects of the ITF patterns that changed over the years were the previous positions or chambers that are found with the movements in the patterns and fundamental techniques.

The soldiers in the military that were developing their Taekwon-Do also made it different from karate by the greater amounts of kicks that they created, along with the height that they were performing them at, as well as the flying or jumping in the air that they emphasized. If one examines the 1960 first edition of a book titled "Karate: the Art of Empty Hand Fighting" by Hidetaka Nishiyama and Richard C. Brown, they will see between 11 and 14 kicks listed, with 2 of them being side kicks. If the alternate directions and attacking tools are added, this number can rise 18 or so kicks. Compare this to the Gen. Choi's second book written on Taekwon-Do in 1965 and there are 26 kicks listed, not counting the additional tools or directions. One can also notice with this book the greater emphasis on combination, consecutive and flying kicks that

General Choi with 29th Infantry Fist Division Flag - Where Taekwon-Do was 1st Developed

were becoming part of the Taekwon-Do syllabus. By the time the 1999 edition of the 15 volume Encyclopedia of Taekwon-Do was written by Gen. Choi, you will see a whole single volume book dedicated to just kicking. In it there are some 96 kicks listed, with 7 of them being side kicks. This list does not include the various tools and direction the same kicks can be performed with.

These soldiers did not just add kicks. They in effect created a mix of the martial arts that were around at the time. The Taekwon-Do developed in the ROK Army was a MMA with the goal of self defense, not a sport. While they paid some attention to the new hyungs and

*Grandmaster Park Jong Soo
One of TKD's Most Important
Pioneers, 1960s*

the old karate katas, a good bulk of their training day was spending hours working with each other, adding what worked and taking out what was not effective for self defense purposes.

Kim Jong Chan, one of the first military Taekwon-Do instructors brought boxing and wrestling to the mix. Rhee Ki Ha, who was the first person Gen. Choi promoted to 9th degree grandmaster learned judo and Sumo wrestling before learning karate. Cho Sang Min, a former chief instructor of the ITF first learned boxing before he started karate. Park Jung Tae, the former chairman of the ITF Instruction Committee, before he went on to found the Global Taekwon-Do Federation did boxing and judo along with karate. Choi Kwang Jo who was another chief instructor of the ITF learned Kwon Bup, which was Korean karate with some Chinese martial art influence. Rhee Chung Chol a pioneer of Taekwon-Do in Australia trained in boxing and other martial arts before joining the military. Choi Nam Sung who was a pioneer who introduced Taekwon-Do to Argentina in 1967 did both Hapkido and boxing. Sgt. Kong Yong Il, who traveled the world promoting Taekwon-Do had trained in Shotokan karate and judo. Dr. Dong Ja Yang was a high ranking black belt instructor in yudo, the Korean name for judo. He taught the throws, falls and takedowns on the first official ITF Training Film. Lee Won Il, who had trained in Hapkido, demonstrates the hoosinsul self defense techniques throughout Gen. Choi's 1972 Taekwon-Do textbook.

Even second generation Taekwon-Do students crossed trained in other martial arts. Grandmaster Van Binh Nyugen, the first Vietnamese student to be promoted to 9th degree black belt by Gen. Choi, trained in several martial arts. In addition to being on the 1964 Judo Olympic team for south Vietnam, he trained in kick boxing, Muy Thai, Aikido and Kendo. Since the military Taekwon-Do was for self defense, it was not only common, but very natural that students would cross train. When one trains for self defense and has elements of realism in their training, it becomes easier to see how martial arts not only have much in common, but it becomes often clearer for the students to see how they often blend together.

GM Van Binh Nuygen, the 1st Vietnamese TKD 9th Dan in Army Uniform. One of only seven Promoted to Grandmaster by General Choi

It is important to understand that the military Taekwon-Do was developed for self defense. It is fairly clear from the above and from talking with and analyzing what has been written about Taekwon-Do in those days, that this was the case. Historical accounts and media reports from the Vietnam War give us evidence that this training was effective. The Republic of Korea was second to the United States in manpower commitment in supporting south Vietnam. The two southern halves of their respective divided countries shared the common enemy of communism. South Korea, by sending troops to fight in the war, was also a way to pay back the support the United States was providing to their country.

Vietnam was also the place where foreign second generation students were first exposed to Taekwon-Do. Vietnamese soldiers like Grandmaster Van Binh and countless American GIs were introduced to Taekwon-Do during their service. The Vietnam War was also the place where the military Taekwon-Do was battle tested. Some accounts of its effectiveness have become legendary, like the Battle of Tra Binh Dong. The exploits of the Korean soldiers was widely reported in many major Korean and English newspapers. Additionally the north Vietnamese communist troops issued a written edict that warned its soldiers to avoid hand to hand combat with the Korean troops because of their Taekwon-Do training.

In 1971, 2000 People Demonstrate Taekwon-Do in Vietnam,
which was one of the first countries outside of Korea and Malaysia to adopt TKD

While it is important to know that military Taekwon-Do was born as a method of self defense, it is equally important to realize that it was a new system that was being formulated under the leadership of Korean Army Gen. Choi. Perhaps the most key point is that these were really the only ones even using the name Taekwon-Do. They of course started its use back in 1954/5, when so ordered by Gen. Choi and Col. Nam to even shout Tae Kwon when saluting in training. So not only was it a specific system that was being organized, it was organized under the name Taekwon-Do, almost exclusively. Only a few outside the military and they were mostly Chung Do Kwan members loyal to Gen. Choi, which used the name Taekwon-Do to describe their Korean martial art. This is all verifed by Dr. Kimm, Dr. Capener, Alex Gillis, Kang and Lee, Grandmaster

General Choi with 29th Infantry Fist Division Patch

Lee Chong Woo and Kim Soo, among others.

There were of course others doing Korean martial arts. We know the five original Kwans which opened in the mid 1940s were also back then doing mostly karate. They however use Korean or Chinese terms by calling it Tang Soo Do, Kong Soo Do and Kwon Bup at that time. Later on other Korean names like Su Bak Do and Hwa Soo Do were also used. These Kwans and the off shoots they spurred all developed slowly and over time in their own ways away from the karate roots. However they were for the most part still doing the karate and the Japanese katas, but were calling them by the Korean term of Pyong Ahn forms.

As stated above, four out of the five original Kwan founders, Lee Won Kuk, Ro Byung Jik, Yoon Byung In and Chun sang Sup tried to unite in some fashion in the late 1940s, to no avail. During the Korean War Dr. Yoon Kwe Byung, who was one of the seven Koreans to have studied martial arts abroad during the occupation, worked with original Kwan founders Ro Byung Jik and Hwang Kee, as well as some emerging second generation leaders to form the Korean Kong Soo Do Association. While this attempt failed as well as Hwang Kee, supported by Ro Byung Jik created the Korean Tang Soo Do Association. Later Hwang Kee also formed the Su bak Do Association.

Gen. Choi and Grandmaster Son Duk Sung led an effort to form the Taekwon-Do Association of Korea in 1957. While that was short lived, Gen. Choi was successful in forming the Korean Taekwon-Do Association in 1959. Grandmaster Hwang Kee soon dropped out. That year was also significant for the military Taekwon-Do as Gen. Choi authored the first book on Taekwon-Do and led a Taekwon-Do military demonstration team abroad for the first time. They performed in both south Vietnam and Taiwan, further cementing the Taekwon-Do name.

Historic 1st TKD Demo Abroad - Vietnam 1959. Led by then VI Dan General Choi and then V Dan Capt. Nam Tae Hi

On May 16, 1961 a military coup occurred in south Korea. The first presidential administration in power from 1948, suffered from accusations of increasing corruption. They were forced out of power and the interim civilian government took over in April of 1960. It however never took hold, as it was replaced by the military coup. The coup was well planned and was successful, not spilling any blood. Historical accounts unrelated to Taekwon-Do report that it even caught the American government by surprise. Few were familiar with Gen. Park Jung Hee, who oversaw the coup. He had the support of many, if not most of the military generals, including Gen. Choi. Gen. Choi repeatedly stated over the years that he only supported the coup as Gen. Park promised to turn the government over to the people.

The issue of politics must be understood to fully understand the complex and confused history of Tae kwon Do. There were hard feelings between the two generals. Apparently Gen. Park was tried and convicted earlier in his Army career by military tribunal. Gen. Choi sat on the court martial panel as a judge who voted for his conviction. However the outbreak of the Korean War gave Gen. Park a second chance and he took advantage of the opportunity to eventually rise to a 2 Star major general. Once in power as head of the country, he consolidated his power by removing ones he did not trust and those that did not fully support him. While it is said that he did not trust Gen. Choi, it was also clear that Gen. Choi was critical of Gen. Park. When you read accounts of history, you will see that Gen. Park forced his opposition out of the military, often sending them abroad as Ambassadors, where they would have little power, say or influence to interfere with his administration. Others were forced into exile and over the years faced fates much worse, with many being imprisoned as political dissidents, beaten or worse, with some disappearing altogether.

In 1962 Gen. Choi himself was sent to Malaysia as an Ambassador. While this served to marginalize him as a political opponent, it also started the wane of the power he held that he yielded in the Taekwon-Do world to get his way. While at his diplomatic post he also introduced Taekwon-Do to Malaysia, the country he often referred to as the second home of Taekwon-Do. One of his first students there was a judo player that Gen. Choi trained in Taekwon-Do. This man Low Koon Lin was honored with promotion to 9th degree grandmaster by the ITF in 2006.

GM Low Koon Lin (Promoted to 9th Dan in 2006 by the ITF) was a White Belt Student of Gen Cho when he was Ambassador to Malaysia 1962 and GM Jhoon Rhee

Gen. Choi sent for retired Army Sgt-Major Kim Bok Man and Woo Jae Lim to come to assist him. While there they helped him to finalize many of the other patterns and helped him with the manuscript for the new Taekwon-Do book he was working on.

After his diplomatic assignment ended in 1964, he returned home to Korea. Once there he saw that the Korean Tae Soo Do Association had replaced the Korean

Taekwon-Do Association he formed in 1959. He worked hard to get elected as this group's third president. Once president he lobbied very hard to get the name changed back to Taekwon-Do. Tae Soo Do was a compromise name offered by Dr. Yoon Kwe Byung. When this group was being formed in 1961, a fight ensued over the name. While Col. Nam and Grandmaster Uhm Won Gyu wanted the name Taekwon-Do, the others refused. They fought for either Kong Soo Do or Tang Soo Do. According to Lee and

Early TaeSooDo Champions, including Park Dong Keun, Ahn Dae Sup of the Ji Do Kwan and Taekwon-Do Choi Chang Keun of the Oh Do Kwan

Kang in their Modern History of Tae Kwon Do, Dr. Yoon offered the name as a compromise, as he saw there would be little movement forward if they could not settle the contentious problem of the name. Tae came from Tae Kwon Do, with Soo from both Kong Soo Do and Tang Soo Do. The Do was shared by all three. So the compromise worked and it was accepted.

In August of 1965, Gen. Choi was able to again make an issue of the name. He was able to win the close vote, which some report by a margin of only one. Gen. Choi used the fact that the Korean government had already approved and was paying for a Kukki Taekwon-Do

1965 Goodwill World Tour

Goodwill tour around the world. In addition, he was printing new English books with the name Taekwon-Do. These books would be distributed on the world tour. So his argument was persuasive, as how could the president of Tae Soo Do lead a Taekwon-Do goodwill tour around the world handing out Taekwon-Do books. This marked a pivotal moment in Taekwon-Do's history, as it was the first time the term Taekwon-Do was accepted by those outside of Gen. Choi's influence and control.

We can see clearly that only the military was using the name Taekwon-Do to describe their Korean martial art for self defense. It is clear to see that the first use of the name outside of Gen. Choi, his soldiers and followers was August of 1965. This was more than 10 years after Gen. Choi named it and received permission and authorization from the president of Korea, Seung Man Rhee. In 1971 Gen. Park, who was still in power as a military dictator, wrote Kukki Tae Kwon Do in calligraphy as well. This prompted more Korean martial artists to adopt the name as well. With the opening of the Kukkiwon in 1972 and the formation of the WTF in 1973, the name became even more widespread. Finally in August of 1978, when the Kwans were numbered and retired, the difficult transition was finalized, with full and complete adoption of the name Tae Kwon Do, some 23 years after Gen. Choi started using it exclusively.

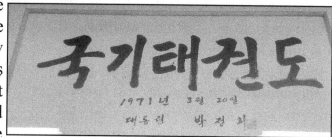

Kukki Taekwon-Do caligraphy by Gen Park Displayed in Kukkiwon

3rd Kukkiwon President Lee Seung Wan, a Ji Do Kwan Grandmaster

While the above tells the story of the increasing use of the name Tae Kwon Do, it does not speak to what these Korean martial artists were doing as far as techniques goes. Now we know that at the start they were all doing a form of Korean karate. While each Kwan moved away from the karate roots in their own way, the Jido Kwan played probably the most pivotal role in developing the sports rules that would become Olympic Taekwondo.

According to Dr. Steve Capener, formerly of the WTF, the rules were adopted to be different from karate. Grandmaster Lee Chong Woo, who I interviewed in 2010 played perhaps the most important role. He was assisted by Grandmaster Uhm Won Gyu of the Chung Do Kwan and Lee Nam Suk of the Chang Moo Kwan. By making these rules, they provided the impetus for the development of Taekwondo as a kicking sport. Once settled as a sport, innovation followed that led to fast counter kicks and quick foot stepping that has become the trademark of sport Taekwondo. Low kicks, grabs, sweeps, hand techniques, other than punch with the forefist to the chest were outlawed. Full contact was required to score a point and the matches were now timed with corner judges. All this was unlike the karate stop match, non-contact point rules in place.

While this was the birth of sport Taekwondo, we must remember that it was first called Tae Soo Do. It was Tae

Master Vitale with WTF Secretary General who has both a USA Criminal Justice background and elected political office (Mayor) at WTF Office

Soo Do that made its first appearance in 1963 at the Korean National Sports Festival. Tae Soo Do was also introduced to sport competitions in school and universities in starting in 1964. While Gen. Choi was able to get the name changed back to Taekwon-Do he could not get them to adopt his system. Because of this contention, he was forced out of the KTA. In an attempt to work together, these second generation leaders helped

Gen Choi and Ji Do Kwan National Champion GM Park Dong Keun

him to form the ITF on March 22, 1966 in Seoul Korea. Grandmasters Lee Chong Woo served as technical director with Uhm Won Gyu serving as the Secretary General.

The first TKD magazine - ITF Human Weapon, 1969 cover

Attempts to consolidate the techniques were not successful. The KTA started to create their own set of forms they called Palgwe. According to Simon John O'Neill and Dr. He Young Kimm the committee consisted of Kwak Kun Sik, Park Hae Man, Hyun Jong Myun, Lee Yong Sup, Lee Kyo Yun and Kim Soon Bae. They worked on devising these new forms between 1965 and 1967. As they were designing these new forms several attempts to combine these forms with the Chang Hon set used by the ITF within a common syllabus were unsuccessful. Both sides argued over the amount each could submit and they were not able to come to an agreement.

Another attempt to get the KTA and the ITF to work together included the merging of some of the top personnel. Gen. Choi was made honorary president of the KTA and Grandmaster Lee Nam Suk was made Secretary General of the ITF. This effort was also not successful. By 1972 Gen. Choi saw he was not only losing his hold over Taekwon-Do, but the brutality of the military dictatorship led by Gen. Park was approaching its height. Professor Bruce Cummings, PhD of Chicago University states that 1972 was the peak of the brutality of the Park regime. Sensing this and seeing it first hand, Gen. Choi decided to exile himself to Canada at the start of 1972. He did this to avoid getting caught up as a political dissident, while at the same time preserving his style and vision of Taekwon-Do. The ITF then voted to relocate their international headquarters to Toronto.

Later that year (1972) the Kukkiwon opened under the leadership of Dr. Kim Un Yong. Dr. Kim had been a savvy political diplomat for the Korean government. He spoke several languages and held important political assignments overseas for Korea at such high profile locations as Washington DC, London and New York City at the United Nations. Dr. Kim was already serving as the 6th president of the KTA since January 23, 1971. Lee and Kang suggest he was selected to help solve some of the problems that Tae Kwon Do had internally. Also in 1972 another committee was formed to create another new set of forms. Bae Young Ki, Lee Chong Woo of the

Dr Kim Un Yong, founder of the WTF and the person most responsible for Olympic Taekwondo, with Master Vitale and Gloria Rhee

Jido Kwan and Han Young Tae a breakaway senior student of the Moo Duk Kwan joined Kwak Kun Sik, Park Hae Man, Hyun Jong Myun, Lee Yong Sup, Lee Kyo Yun and Kim Soon Bae, the same six who had earlier developed the Palgwe forms. This was important as it allowed the input of these men and their Kwans. It also signified the break from the first generation founders and leaders, as Gen. Choi, Dr. Yoon and Grandmaster Hwang Kee remained apart from this movement which was focusing on turning Tae Kwon Do into a martial sport.

The martial art leaders of this movement were Grandmaster Lee Chong Woo, Uhm Won Gyu and Lee Nam Suk, aided by the above listed grandmasters that assisted in creating the two sets of the forms that they would utilize over the years. These martial artists were led by Dr. Kim Un Yong, who garnered the necessary government support and had the political skills required to navigate the international sports community. These are the Korean men who should be thanked for making Taekwondo a martial sport that was so successful that it gained official Olympic sport status. They in effect can be viewed as the team that founded Kukki Taekwondo. What also needs to be made clear is that most of these leaders initially rejected the name Taekwon-Do and instead preferred the Korean karate names or the compromise name of Tae Soo Do. However, once they accepted the name, they put their own mark on making Taekwondo a new martial sport.

Gen. Choi often claimed that these others Taekwondo men used the name he came up with. He even went as far to say that they were not Taekwon-Do, but karate. Well as you can see the truth is that Gen. Choi actually forced them with the pressure he exerted in 1965 to change the name from Tae Soo Do to Taekwon-Do. If he did not lead that effort, or if he was simply not successful, this controversy would not exist today. Gen. Choi would have led the International Taekwon-Do Federation that oversees the Korean martial art of self defense. Dr. Kim and Grandmaster Lee would have led the World Tae Soo Do Federation which would have overseen the Korean martial sport. That sport of Tae Soo Do would have been in the Olympics and not Taekwon-Do.

As to the claims that the WTF was karate, that has an element of truth to it. The exact same claim can be said of Gen. Choi and his Taekwon-Do as well. In fact it was often stated by his detractors. Truth be told, their roots came from karate. This is simply fact and can not be refuted. However, sadly neither side would acknowledge the work the other did to move from and develop away from those common karate roots. The ITF did it first in the military as a mix of the fighting systems available at the time. They continued with the new Korean patterns they developed, along with the innovative kicks and flying techniques, along with their distinctive way of moving vertically to increase power and make their art flow. Of course the WTF did it with the new sports rules they developed that eventually led to new fast kicks and super quick stepping, making their martial sport a unique kick-counter kick activity unlike any other martial art or sport.

During a 2010 interview with Lt. Col. Lee Sang Ku he explains what happens next and helps us to understand how the political ramifications affected Gen. Choi and Tae Kwon Do. Col. Lee was also a former Ambassador and deputy director of the KCIA. He at one time also went by the name of Lee Kew Hoon, before he changed it to Sang Ku. Ambassador Lee was a military academy classmate of Col. Nam. He was also an early instructor of Taekwon-Do in the military. He assisted Gen. Choi with the legal research needed to form an international organization. He is also the one who came up with the names for the ITF and WTF.

Ambassador Lee says Gen. Choi was obsessed with Taekwon-Do. It was all he wanted to talk about when he woke in the morning. He speculates that Gen. Choi along the way not only burned people with his leadership style, but also may have disappointed his superiors as he was an Army general and then an Ambassador and all he wanted to work on was Taekwon-Do. He went on to say that it was mandatory for all Korean men to serve in the military. At a time there were approximately 700,000 soldiers in the Army, many of who had been exposed to Gen. Choi and his Taekwon-Do over the years. Ambassador Lee said that it was not inconceivable that some in the government may have become uneasy as thousands of troops each month were discharged, many of whom would have some allegiance to Gen. Choi.

Likewise the civilian Kwans were small in number and did not have anywhere near the amount of students that the military did. As a result, many of the Tae Soo Do and civilian gym leaders were lacking the power, influence and control Gen. Choi had. Grandmaster Kim Young Soo estimates that some 60% of the civilian gyms were doing the Chang Hon set of patterns, while everyone in the military was. In addition, Gen. Choi started to voice more opposition to the direction the country was taking and Gen. Park's refusal to hand over the government to the people. The military dictator started cutting back on many freedoms and was increasing human rights abuses as he maintained strict control over the government. Now some like Dr. Murphy Song, PhD and professor of Economics describe that many actions were needed as Korea was in turmoil, facing constant threat from the communists. Many look back on the administration of Gen. Park as what led Korea to its economic success of today.

Ambassador Lee said that once Gen. Choi exiled himself he became an even louder critic of the Park regime. While Ambassador Lee tried to talk to Gen. Choi, he refused to come home and eventually engaged in more "anti-nationalist activity". The height of this was in 1980 when Gen. Choi crossed the border into the Democratic People's Republic of (north) Korea to introduce Taekwon-Do there. While Gen. Choi may have merely done this for the sake of sharing and spreading Taekwon-Do, his act and subsequent outreach and embrace of north Korea was viewed as treason. Many called him a communist and a traitor. Over the next couple of years, the few remaining loyal Korean masters that had weathered the bribes, pressure, threats and more of the KCIA and the south Korean dictatorships to leave the ITF, finally did walk away from Gen. Choi. This weakened his position and gave new ammunition for his detractors to use against him and they did.

7th International ITF Demo Team, 1980 north Korea
(Photo Courtesy of Team Member Master Dimitrios Kosmoglou - far right)

Standing room only audience in historic 1980 demo, introducing Taekwon-Do to north Korea
(Photo Courtesy of Team Member Master Dimitrio)

Gen Choi and his son, Jung Hwa reunite with family in north Korea, 1980

Through the support that north Korea gave to Gen. Choi and the ITF, the ITF was able to regroup and grow. However the stigma and label of communist or north Korean Taekwon-Do grew. Today in south Korea, ITF Taekwon-Do is viewed that way. It is difficult for an ITF Dojang to survive in many areas of south Korea because of this unfair stigma. In fact, few in south Korea have heard of Gen. Choi or know the ITF was formed there in 1966. They are under the mistaken impression that it is from north Korea. It is a shame that Gen. Choi's accomplishments have been so tainted over the years because of politics. Few know of his award by Canada for his peace efforts through Taekwon-Do or that he was nominated for a Nobel Peace Prize for those same efforts. Hopefully his outreach to the north through Taekwon-Do, will be viewed in the same light as his efforts were in other communist and socialist countries, to which the WTF followed him to as well.

Historic discussion with ITF pioneers and WTF President Choue, with WTF Sect. Gen. Yang and Public Relations Director Kang looking on

Millions of people around the world in 191 nations now practice an activity that they call Tae Kwon Do. While there are some differences between those that train, they also share many things in common as well, including the same history. This history all started in the same time and place. However over time, it was developed along many roads, which included two main paths that we have come to know as ITF and WTF. Tae Kwon Do, Taekwon-Do or Taekwondo, our history is the same, up to a point. So when we learn the true history, we can see our common bond that we share. Hopefully the present generation and those that will come in the future will understand this and embrace each other more. If that happens, Tae Kwon Do will flourish and its students will reap the benefits.

Reference Sources

Abernethy, I. (2010) Website
Anslow, S. A. (2006) Chang Hon Taekwon-Do Hae Sul
Armstrong, C. (2007) Personal Interview Columbia Universities Asian Studies Department Chairman
Capener, S. (1995) Problems in the Identity and Philosophy of Taegwondo and Their Historical Causes, Korea journal
Choi, C. K. (2007) The Korean Martial Art of Tae Kwon Do and Early History
Choi, H. H. (1959) Taekwon-Do
Choi, H. H. (1965) Taekwon-Do
Choi, H. H. (1972) Taekwon-Do
Choi, H. H. (1999) Encyclopedia of Taekwon-Do
Choi, H. H. (2000) Taekwon-Do and I, Volumes 1, 2 and 3
Cook, D. (2006) Traditional Taekwondo: Core Techniques, History and Philosophy
Culin, S. (1895) Korean Games
Culture and Tourism Ministry of The Republic of Korea (2000) Taekwondo: The Spirit Of Korea
Della Pia, J. A. (1994) Korea's Muye Dobo Tongji, Journal of Asian Martial Arts
Education Ministry of The Republic of Korea
Gillis, A. (2008) A Killing Art: The Untold History of Tae Kwon Do
Gillis, A. (2009) Personal Interview and Subsequent Correspondence
Hancock, J. (1995) The Truth About Pyong Ahn Hyung

Hawkins, P. (2006) Interview of Grandmaster Kim Young Soo, TKD and the Korean Martial Arts

Hawkins, P. (2009) Interview of Grandmaster Lee Yoo Sun, Totally Tae Kwon Do Magazine

Heron, M. (1999) Interview of Choi Hong Ho, The Times

Horton, N. (2005) Japanese Martial Arts

International Taekwon-Do Federation (1974) Official Training Film

Kang, S. L. (1997) Interview of Grandmaster Lee Won Kuk, Taekwondo Times Magazine

Kang, W. S. and Lee, K. M. (1999) Modern History of Taekwondo

Kim Un Yong (2010) Personal Interview Conducted in Seoul Korea

Kimm, H.Y. (2000) Interview of Choi Hong Hi, Taekwondo Times Magazine

Kimm, H.Y. (2008) History of Korean and Hapkido

Kimm, H.Y. (2006-2010) Personal Interviews and Correspondence over a 4 year period.

Kukkiwon Textbook (2006) published by the World Taekwondo Headquarters (Kukkiwon)

Lee, C. W. (2010) Personal Interview, Seoul Korea

Lee, K. (2008) Personal Interview and Correspondence, National Committee on North Korea, Washington, DC

Lee, S. W. (2010) Personal Interview of Kukkiwon President, Kukkiwon, Seoul Korea

Lee, S. K. (2010) Personal Interview, Seoul Korea

Losik, L. (1997) Moo Duk Kwan: Miracle or Mistake? Taekwondo Times Magazine (From his work on review of The History of the Moo Duk Kwan by Founder and Grandmaster Hwang Kee)

McLain, R. (2006) Korean Karate History: Why all the Confusion? An Interview with Grandmaster Kim Pyung Soo

McLain, R. (2006) Master Yoon Byung In's Legacy: The ChangMoo Kwan and KangDuk Kwan

Nilsen, O. (2009) Debunking the Muye Dobo Tongji, Totally Tae Kwon Do Magazine

Nishiyama, H. and Brown, R. C. Karate: The Art of Empty Hand Fighting

O'Neill, S. J. (2008) The Taeguek Cipher: The Patterns of Kukki Taekwondo as a Practical Self defense Syllabus

Park Jong Soo (2006-2010) Personal Interview and Subsequent Correspondence

Pederson, M. and Rubbeling, H. (English and German Translators of) (1984) Television Interview of Taek Kyon Master Song Duk Ki for Culture Seminar (a Korean TV Show)

Perez, H. (1998) Traditional vs. Sport: Will the Real Taekwondo Stand Up Black Belt Magazine

Republic of Korea Embassy to the United States Website (2010)

Rosenbaum, M. (2002) The Fighting Arts: Their Evolution from Secret Societies to Modern Times

Scott, S. (2003) Taekwondo Basics

Scott, S. (2006) Advanced Taekwondo

Song Moo Kwan Website (2010)

Song, M. (2006- 2009) Personal Interview and Correspondence

Terrigno, C. (2007) The Moo Duk Kwan Story, Tang Soo Do World (From their work on review of The History of the Moo Duk Kwan by Founder and Grandmaster Hwang Kee, 1995)

United States Department of State Website (2010)

Van Binh, N. (2007) Personal Interview and Subsequent Correspondence

Wall, R. (2001?) Interview of Choi Hong Hi

Weiss, E. Interview of Col. Nam Tae Hi, Taekwondo Times Magazine

World Taekwondo Federation Website (2010)

Yi, D. M., Pak D. S. and Park J. G. (Army Generals) (1790) Muye Dobo Tongji: The Comprehensive Illustrated Manual of Martial Arts of Ancient Korea. English Translation Kim, S. H. (2000)

Yook S. C. (2002) Interview of Grandmaster Lee Chong Woo, Shin Dong A Magazine

Young, R. (1993) The History and Development of Tae Kyon, Journal of Asian Martial Arts

Yung, O. (1997) The Elevation of Taekkyon from Folk Game to Martial Art, Journal of Asian Martial Arts

I have tried my best to be as complete and honest as I could be, given what my extensive research has found, regardless of my own personal beliefs or what I was led to believe before I engaged in serious academic investigative research. I have listed the sources that have contributed more directly to this essay. I have not listed all the interviews I have conducted, nor all the sources (my own personal library is now well over 100 sources) I have consulted or Pioneers and Tae Kwon Do leaders I have trained under or been exposed to in my almost 40 years of martial arts education that has now spanned 5 different decades. Please feel free to contact me through the author of this book, Mr. Stuart Anslow or directly at *TKD.Research@yahoo.com* if I have left anything out, been remiss or if you may have some additional information. It is only through this type of cooperative effort that we can hope to make the history of Tae Kwon Do and its development both more complete and more truthful. Thank you!

Performers Biographies

Gordon Slater, 6th Degree

Gordon started Taekwon-Do in February, 1983 with the UKTA (United Kingdom Taekwon-Do Association), gaining his 1st degree in August 1987 with the TAGB (Tae Kwon Do Association of Great Britain) after waiting a year longer to grade due to transferring associations.

Gaining his 6th degree with the GTI (Global Taekwon-Do International) in October, 2009 he has, on his journey been the 1995 GTI English patterns and destruction champion, as well as consistently winning gold medals in patterns and destruction throughout the 90's.

During his time in Taekwon-Do he has been part of various Taekwon-Do organisations such as the UKTA (United Kingdom Taekwon-Do Association), TAGB Tae Kwon Do Association of Great Britain), ITS (Independent Taekwondo Schools) but is happy with his current association the GTI (Global Taekwon-Do International) where he is Grading Examiner, qualified referee and umpire. He has also trained in Wing-Chun Kung Fu, Karate, Kick Boxing and Boxing.

I first met Gordon around 2003 at a tournament in Kent, UK, one that we went to many times over the years, both as instructors and competitors. Indeed we have both fielded students against each other in the various divisions, as well as competed against each other in patterns, sparring and destruction divisions over the years. I asked him to be part of these books because of my high regards for him, both as a person and due to his skills in Taekwon-Do.

Gordon demonstrates the patterns Yong-Gae, So-San, Se-Jong and Tong-Il. More information on Gordon can be found at *www.essextkd.co.uk*

Stuart Anslow, 5th Degree

Stuart started Taekwon-Do early in 1991 under David Bryan (now 6th degree) and

John Pepper (who has now retired from Taekwon-Do). He graded his kup grades with the BUTF (British United Taekwon-Do Federation), gaining his 1st degree in 1994. He continued with the BUTF (which rejoined the ITF for a period) through to 2nd degree before parting ways and going solo. During this solo period he established his school; *Rayners Lane Taekwon-do Academy* in 1999, as well as taking his 3rd degree in 2000, 4th degree in 2005, before finally achieving his current grade of 5th degree in 2010 under legendary Taekwon-Do pioneer, Master Willie Lim, 8th degree.

Having had a good career in competition, culminating in World gold and silver medals in 2000, his main focus has been running his school and promoting Taekwon-Do. Further information can be found in the 'About The Author' section of this book or at the academy web site *www.raynerslanetkd.com*

Stuart demonstrates the patterns Yul-Gok, Juche, Sam-Il, Yoo-Sin, Choi-Yong, Pyong-Hwa, Ul-Gi, Moon-Moo and Sun-Duk.

Elliott Walker, 3rd Degree

Elliott started Taekwon-Do in 1989, aged 15, where he trained with Mr Brian Williams (6th degree) the senior instructor for the TAGB clubs in the North West of England. When just a 7th kup he joined the British Army, but continued training whenever he could at various clubs around the UK gaining excellent experience of the various associations and clubs. He continued to grade through the kup ranks within the TAGB up to 2nd kup, being graded by such TAGB notables as Master Don Atkins, Master Ron Sergiew, Master Kenny Walton and Dorian Bytom, before taking his 1st kup with his original instructor Brian Williams, with the (then) newly formed North West TaeKwonDo.

Achieving his 1st degree in 1996, he then started instructing and continued to grade up to his present rank of 3rd degree, which he achieved in 2005.

Having been posted to Germany in 1993 whilst with the British Army, he trained with a WTF club for a year which enabled him to practice and learn the way the WTF like to kick, again improving his overall knowledge of Taekwon-Do. In 1998 he visited Canada whilst with the army, training at local ITF style clubs to increase his skills further.

When the British Army formed the AMAA (Army Martial Arts Association), he was selected for the British Army team and remained a team member until he left the forces, being awarded Army Colours every year for this achievement. Whilst in the British Army team he was both patterns and sparring champion several times and helped the Army Team to become Inter-Service Champions over several different years. Elliott left the army in 2002 to further his Taekwon-Do instruction and now teaches 5 times a week at his schools in Kent, UK.

I first met Elliott at the 'Kick It' tournaments in 2000. I recall at the time, someone told me my next competitor in the black belt sparring was on the Army Taekwon-Do squad, so I was thinking it was going to be a heavy contact, rough and tough type of bout. Much to my surprise, Elliott was more a classy fighter and didn't go the snot and blood route as he didn't need to and it made the bout a great game of 'cat and mouse'. Over the years we have competed on numerous occasions and our friendship truly underlines one of my sayings (regarding competitions) of: *'2 minutes of war, friends for life'*. A tough fighter and a great technician - these are the reasons I asked Elliott to be part of these books.

Elliott demonstrates pattern Ko-Dang. More information on Elliott can be found at *www.kent-taekwondo.co.uk*

Vikram Gautam, 3rd Degree

Vikram started Taekwon-Do when he was just aged 10 years old (in 1991). As a child he trained with my instructors Mr. David Bryan, 6th Degree and Mr. John Pepper, 2nd Degree at Wembley Taekwon-Do School, which was part of the BUTF (British United Taekwon-do Federation). He continued to train at this Wembley Taekwon-Do School under the exceptional guidance of Mr. David Bryan and Mr. John Pepper for the next 9 years achieving his 1st degree in 2000. Following his 1st degree he began assisting me at Rayners Lane Taekwon-Do Academy and eventually started training there full time due to university making it impossible to train at his former club due to conflicts in times. Vikram graded to 2nd degree in March 2006 and for 3rd degree in 2010 under legendary Taekwon-Do pioneer, Master Willie Lim, 8th degree.

I remember Vikram as a child student who was always inquisitive and eager to learn new stuff, so much so it seems he used to ask me to teach him a new kick every class. When he first competed as a blue belt, he stole the golds in both patterns and sparring and has continued in a similar vein ever since. Following his 1st degree, he competed and fought a Karate black belt who had turned his hand to Taekwon-Do and the fight ended within about 3 seconds as Vikram landed a superb flying back piercing kick as his first technique, which although controlled, hit his opponent straight in the face ending it as a TKO! Vikram's superb natural ability and technique is why I asked him to be part of these books.

Vikram demonstrates the patterns Do-San, Toi-Gye, Choong-Moo, Jee-Goo and Eui-Am.

Colin Avis, 2nd Degree

Colin began practicing Taekwon-Do in 2001 at Rayners Lane Academy and has trained there ever since. After around five years of training he attained the grade of 1st Degree in 2006. Having reached the coveted black belt ranks, Colin maintained the same work ethic he displayed during his formative coloured belt years up to 1st degree, swiftly achieving the rank of 2nd Degree in 2008. Colin was the first student of Rayners Lane Taekwon-Do Academy to be promoted all the way from 10th Kup to 2nd Degree.

Although a student of the Academy, Colin also assists in teaching and has done so for a number of years. He can always be seen supporting the Academy's endeavours in hosting and attending numerous seminars, tournaments etc. Colin is also a seasoned competitor himself and has won his fair share of silverware, with one of the highlights being a silver medal won for sparring at the world championships hosted by Grandmaster Hee Il Cho. He was also part of the Rayners Lane Men Sparring Team that took the silver at the same World Championships.

Colin has won more 'Student of the Month' awards than any other student, as well a being the only Academy student to ever have been named 'Student of the Year' on more than one occasion, winning it in both 2004 and 2007. Colin's passion for the art, commitment and consistency to both training and the Academy as well as his technical skills are why I asked him to be part of these books.

Colin demonstrates Saju Jirugi and Saju Tulgi, as well as patterns Won-Hyo, Hwa-rang, Ge-Baek, Choong-Jang and Jook-Am.

Lyndsey Reynolds, 2nd Degree

Lyndsey started training in Taekwon-do at Rayners Lane Academy in 2000, gaining her 1st Degree in March 2008 and in doing so, became the first female student to attain a dan grade at the Academy. She became the Academy's 'Student of the Year' in 2002 and still trains as diligently as she always has. Lyndsey graded for 2nd degree in 2011.

As a white belt, her first ever competition was a World Championships in 2000 and since then she has had a good competition career and is a fearsome fighter. Her most notable tournament success was at the 2004 World Championships where she achieved a gold in sparring, a silver in patterns and a further gold as part of the Rayners Lane female team in the team sparring division.

At Rayners Lane all students are equal and thus the girls mix it up with the boys which has transcended further for Lyndsey over the years with a memorable moment being when she was a yellow belt and there were no other ladies entered in her sparring division. The event organiser gave her the choice of a straight gold or fighting in the mens division. She chose the latter and despite some tough opponents took the bronze! This happened again recently as a black belt as well! Lyndsey's skills, guts and steadfast determination is why I asked her to be part of these books.

Lyndsey demonstrates the Silla Knife Form.

Parvez Sultan, 1st Degree

Parvez started Taekwon-Do in January 2000 at Rayners Lane Academy. Always training hard, he achieved his 1st degree in 2006 along side 'Slumdog Millionaire' start Dev Patel amongst others, making them the first students of the Academy to go from white to black belt. He also won the Academy's 'Student of the Year' award in 2001.

Parvez has had a good competition career winning many medals along the way, with his highlights being the World Championships in 2004 where, after a terrible first day at the event, he pulled it together for day 2 and won the combined middle and heavyweight brown/red belt sparring division, fighting some tremendous fighters along the way. One of his proudest moments was testing himself at the authors previous organisations tournament (the BUTF British Championships) and winning the gold in the mens senior kup division after many good fights, actually ending up facing a club mate in the finals who had come up on the other side of the table.

Through the years Parvez has been a dedicated student throughout the years, training hard and showing good skills and technique, which is why I asked him to be part of these books.

Parvez demonstrates the patterns Jee-Sang and Po-Eun.

Sushil Punj, 1st Degree

Sushil started Taekwon-Do at the Academy in 1999 at just 8 years old. After achieving his 2nd Kup he took a hiatus from training, returning to take his 1st Kup, before taking his 1st degree in April, 2009 at just 17 years old. He has competed in both national and international tournaments including a World Championships in 2004.

As a child student, Sushil unfortunately failed his 2nd kup grading and stopped training, as many young students do after such disappointments, however, unlike others he showed true indomitable spirit by resuming training a few years later being older and wiser, with a brand new and intense focus taking him passed the grading he previously failed and to 1st degree, making him one of the few black belts to have come from the Academy which are the reasons I asked Sushil to be part of these books.

Sushil demonstrates the patterns Chon-Ji, Dhan-Goon, Joong-Gun and Kwang-Gae.

Kate Barry, 1st Kup

Kate started training at Rayners Lane Taekwon-do Academy just after it was founded in April 1999 and has trained there ever since. At the time of writing these books, Kate was a 2nd kup. Now a 1st kup and due to take her black belt grading 2011, despite a nagging knee problem that has slowed her progress down.

Kate has competed in many tournaments over the years including two World Championships where she won a silver in points sparring, a bronze in continuous sparring and a gold as part of the women's team in the open grade team sparring divisions, but her most memorable moment comes from a competition when she was an 8th kup where, following a previous training session that involved practising front leg side kicks to score quickly, she employed what she had practised in extra time and as soon as the ref said 'sijak' she hit her opponent with the technique, not only scoring the winning point but also lifting them off the floor and back with the kick.

Kate is the longest 'still in training' student from the Academy, having been there from the early days. Always supportive of the Academy, a hard worker and a long term student are the reasons I asked Kate to be part of these books.

Kate features in the *'Differences Between Organisations'* section of the book, as well as being one of the main photographers.

Marek Handzel, 1st Kup

Marek started Taekwon-Do in September 2004 before joining Rayners Lane Taekwon-Do Academy in February 2005. At the time of writing these books he was a 2nd Kup. He is now a 1st kup and due to take his black belt grading in 2011.

His favourite achievement to date is achieving the *'Student of the year'* award in 2006. Marek has been an exceptional student throughout the years and truly epitomises the tenet of 'perseverance', which is why I asked him to be part of these books.

Marek demonstrates pattern Dan-Gun.

Jonathan Choi, 1st Kup

Jonathan started training at Rayners Lane Taekwon-Do Academy in 2007 and at the time of writing these books he was a 2nd Kup. He is now a 1st kup and due to take his black belt grading in 2011.

A highlight of his training so far was taking home two golds at his first ever tournament. As well as Taekwon-Do Jonathan has a passion for Wushu and was also part of the WTF for a short period whilst in China. Jonathan has also won the Academy's *'Student of the Year'* award in 2008. Jonathan trains hard and is a consummate student which is why I asked him to be part of these books.

Jonathan demonstrates Saju Makgi.

Richard Baker, 1st Kup

Richard started training at Rayners Lane Taekwon-Do Academy in December, 2006 and at the time of writing these books he was a 2nd Kup. He is now a 1st kup and due to take his black belt grading in 2011.

Richard has a good competition record so far, bringing home golds in both patterns and sparring divisions. Richard always gives 110% in training and is a good student which is why I asked him to be part of these books. Richard is due to take his black belt in 2011.

Richard features in the *'Differences Between Organisations'* section of the book.

Lightning Source UK Ltd.
Milton Keynes UK
UKHW050837230119

336057UK00007B/311/P